Earth Changes, Human Destiny

Marko Pogačnik, born in 1944 in Kranj, Slovenia, studied sculpture and acquired an international reputation in conceptual and landscape art. He has developed this further into 'earth lithopuncture', which aims at healing disturbed landscapes and power points. He leads seminars in earth healing in several countries and provides advice on landscape matters for communities and businesses. Marko Pogačnik is a lecturer at the Hagia Chora School for Geomancy, which was founded in 1995.

Earth Changes, Human Destiny is the fourth of Marko's book published by Findhorn Press. We also recommend that you read *Nature Spirits & Elemental Beings, Healing the Heart of the Earth* and *Christ Power and the Earth Goddess*.

Also by the author

Nature Spirits & Elemental Beings
Healing the Heart of the Earth
Chirst Power and the Earth Goddess

(all published by Findhorn Press)

Earth Changes, Human Destiny

coping and attuning with the help
of the Revelation of St John

by Marko Pogačnik

edited by Tony Mitton

FINDHORN
Press

First published in English by Findhorn Press 2000

ISBN 1 899171 53 3

British Library Cataloguing-in-Publication Data.
A catalogue record for this book is available from
the British Library.

Library of Congress Catalog Card Number: 00-105098

Edited by Tony Mitton
Cover design by Thierry Bogliolo
Picture of the Earth © Corbis Images
Cosmogram from a sculpture by Marko Pogačnik
Set in Garamond ITC by Thierry Bogliolo

Printed and bound by WS Bookwell, Finland

Published by
Findhorn Press

The Park, Findhorn
Forres IV36 3TY
Scotland, UK
tel 01309 690582
fax 01309 690036

P. O. Box 13939
Tallahassee
Florida 32317-3939, USA
tel 850 893 2920
fax 850 893 3442

e-mail: info@findhornpress.com
findhornpress.com

Contents

I dedicate this book to some of the most important teachers on my path: my dear wife Marika, our daughters Ajra and Ana, and my companion who has supported me through the most difficult times, William Bloom.

Glossary

Chakras (or front chakras)

The seven main power centers, or vital-energy organs, of the human body, located vertically along the spine.

Geomancy

The word 'geomancy' is derived from 'ge' (Greek) — the earth — and 'manteia' (Greek) — prophecy. Since the end of the 19th century the word has been used in the sense of interaction with the forces of the earth.

Holon

In geomancy theconcept of 'holon', derived from the Greek word for 'whole', denotes a spatial unit that represents a closed energy field. One can speak of a personal or garden holon, local holon, landscape holon, continental or planetary holon.

Sigil

An identifying seal or symbol.

Introduction

It is hard to believe, yet the experience gathered during my earth healing work confirms that the Earth has changed almost completely during the years 1998-2000. The change has occurred in all her dimensions — though the least affected is the only level that we are accustomed to watch carefully, the physical level.

And here is the challenge that this book is addressing: the challenge of the renewed earth cosmos that is already pulsating all around us. But we are members of a civilization that is addicted to the physical plane of existence, and we neither notice nor perceive that anything much is new. We continue to think, feel and act according to our accustomed patterns, ignoring the fantastic possibilities offered by the vibrating and now fully awakened earth consciousness.

I was also one who didn't realize what is going on with our planet now, at the threshold of the new millennium, but I have been shaken awake through strange geomantic experiences, alarm calls transmitted by my dreams, and messages received by my daughters Ana Pogacnik and Ajra Miska from the angelic consciousness. Once I had accepted the inner call and started to observe everything that is changing in me and all around me, the evidence of a unique transformation process accumulated rapidly. Due to my worldwide work in the area of earth healing and geomancy, I had sufficient opportunities to gather relevant, confirmatory experiences on the etheric, emotional, spiritual and even physical levels.

What we can next expect is that the changes, which are almost complete on the inner levels of the planet, will gradually appear in our tangible reality. This might happen by way of a rather dramatic irruption of the new reality, and this would demand that at least a certain percentage of the world population should be consciously alert and also have spiritual tools to rely on while they try to collaborate with the flow of changes. Otherwise these could overrun us.

The purpose of this book accordingly is:

- To offer my personal experiences and insights concerning the changes, to be a mirror in which readers can recognize and understand their own intuitions, dreams and perceptions.

- To present the Revelation of St. John decoded, as a perfect key which has been given to humanity in good time to ensure that we do not get lost in the labyrinth of the recent earth changes.

- To offer exercises to help our personal attunement to the newly emerging powers and qualities; exercises for the perception of the invisible dimensions of reality; and meditations and group rituals to help the process of the earth changes go forward more smoothly.

- To introduce geomancy as a universal language through which it is possible to communicate with worlds and dimensions beyond the physical. We will desperately need such a language if we are not to find ourselves complete strangers among the different aspects and beings of the emerging multi-dimensional earth cosmos.

Even though living with my family in Slovenia — a country formerly belonging to Yugoslavia — I have written several books in German. Some of them have later been translated into English, but this is the first one to have been written in English. I am grateful to Karin and Thierry from Findhorn Press for their trust in the inner purpose of my work and for inviting me to write in a foreign language. Also I am grateful to Tony Mitton for his art in making my English enjoyable for non-Slovenian readers.

Marko Pogačnik
Sempas, April 17th 2000

Chapter One

Earth Changes in Review

At the end of November 1999, at the threshold of the new millennium, I paid a visit to Sao Paulo in Brazil. Can you imagine how a vast landscape, filled with all that a city has to offer — the dwelling place of 20 million living souls — can survive even when there is no way it can breathe properly? Blocks of houses alternate with groups of skyscrapers, composing a dense artificial structure which extends for miles and miles. Nature has no place to breathe. Even the parks have been artificially landscaped to conform to their urban mandates, the main one being to provide people with opportunities for fun and recreation. To perceive the quality of the ground radiation, I bounced[1] my left hand to the ground again and again while waiting at the various underground stations on my way to the city center. I wanted to know how the structure of this endless city was impacting the life forces. I found there was really nothing there to feel. The life force should rise high above one's head — a quality I have found in virgin forests and other environments wholly impregnated by Nature. But not here in the rationally structured megalopolis of Sao Paulo. There, the prevailing sense is that the life force is exhausted and has turned into a thin layer of vibrations which could break down at any moment to reveal the abyss of death.

And yet a hidden surprise was awaiting me. When I walked into the very core of the town with my host Franklin and came out among the trees planted on the square in front of the cathedral, a busy place called 'Se', he suddenly exclaimed, "There is a wall here!" During the last few years I have had occasion to train him

---

1 This describes the action of testing the ground radiation by lowering the hand towards the ground, moving it loosely up and down and then giving it freedom to follow the pattern of radiation.

to perceive the invisible dimensions of life. He organizes my annual workshops and talks in Brazil, and so we often travel together through the country and have the opportunity to exchange our experiences of the subtle levels of particular places and landscapes. So I had good reason to trust his perceptions and check for myself what phenomenon was to be found in the middle of the noisy square. I paused for a moment, took my consciousness deep inside and down to the center of my being, closed my eyes and 'looked'. I could hardly believe that I was perceiving correctly. I saw a pillar composed of subtle but firm vibrations having the quality of white crystal light. It made an abrupt contrast to the chaotic rhythms of the people crossing the square, and the exceptionally poor vitality of the square itself. So I went inside the 'pillar', which had a diameter of approximately 10 meters, and moved my hand through its space in order to feel the atmosphere of the place with my body, and also to listen to its emotional essence.

There could be no doubt. The perfect quality of the light pillar was precisely the same as those I had encountered in several places in Europe, where they had appeared after February 10, 1998. This was the date when I experienced the earth changes starting to manifest. I could recognize their similarity from the way my hand tended to describe a perfect circle in the air, moving in slow motion after I had willed it to move freely in accordance with the emotional quality of the place. But the similarity does not lie only in the circular movement; for even more characteristic of this new geomantic[g] phenomenon is the sensation which accompanies it: one of eternal beauty. I used to describe such 'pillars' as the invisible hands of Heaven on Earth. They seem to have grown out of the earth and yet at the same time channel the noblest impulses from the universe.

Exploring Sao Paulo's cityscape further, I found a few more such 'islands of perfect light'. It became obvious that the threat of a complete breakdown in the life quality of the place is being counter-balanced by a composition of light pillars which maintain

---

g *Throughout this book, the letter 'g' indicates that this concept is introduced for the first time and that there is a definition of this word in the Glossary on page 8.*

and reinforce stability within the turmoil of the much weakened life-organism. The earth is obviously busy disseminating self-healing forces to prevent her existing force-systems from breaking apart, and also to provide a firm base around which new layers of reality can be built during the course of the earth changes[2].

Yet this was not the only hopeful phenomenon that I perceived that day in Sao Paulo, which is surely one of the most difficult urban environments imaginable. Wherever I paused to test the radiation streaming from the ground — using the procedure described above — I became aware that it had two faces. On the one hand I could perceive the extreme impoverishment of the life forces emanating from the ground, due to the suffocating conditions that do not allow the underlying nature organism to breathe. On the other hand, if I concentrated on the element of air and then bounced my hand towards the ground to perceive the quality of the ground radiation, my hand would correctly draw an upward rising spiral: the sign of the undisturbed presence of the life force. How can one understand this surprising contradiction?

Even though what follows may at first sound confusing, the fact is that ever since February 1998 I have perceived two faces of reality existing as if parallel to one another. On the one hand I am aware of the turbulent and unstable conditions of the 'old earth' with which we are all well acquainted. Its presence is marked by the scars and traumas imprinted upon it during millennia of human evolution and specifically through the exceptional aggressiveness of the last century. I am referring not only to the obvious ecological destruction visible all around us, but also to the emotional imprints of human suffering, whether this was experienced in wars, or during the period of third-world colonization, or through the still ongoing suppression of human rights.

On the other hand, since February 10th, 1998, I have experienced another parallel reality. I believe this is in the process of manifesting itself and will become the leading reality of our future. One can recognize it by another kind of radiation emanating from the ground, a kind of radiation which since that day in

---

2 I have already written about these earth changes in the 14th chapter of my book, *Christ Power and the Earth Goddess*, Findhorn Press 1999.

February 1998 I have experienced in many different countries and different continents. It has a special fresh and undamaged quality which can be easily distinguished from the radiation of the 'old earth'. As already mentioned, its characteristics can be depicted as a spiral or identified with the quality of the air element.

At this point you may be asking yourself who I am, and where do I get the authority to make such far-reaching statements. The experience to which I referred above has been distilled from twenty years of concentrated work on earth healing and in geomantic research into sites and landscapes. At the end of the seventies I started to experiment with a kind of earth acupuncture, and a few years later established my own method which I call 'lithopuncture'. Lithopuncture means the positioning of stone pillars on a landscape's acupuncture points in order to stimulate the ecological healing of the place. The lithopuncture stones are attuned to each other to form a network. Their effect is also complemented by signs called 'cosmograms' which I carve onto their surface. Within these signs is encoded the essence of the corresponding site, which supports the healing process on the emotional and spiritual levels.

To locate acupuncture points and position the lithopuncture stones accurately, I had to develop my personal sensitivity to the earth's life forces which compose its invisible geomantic organism. But such sensitivity is of little use if one does not understand the landscape's underlying multidimensionality. So I naturally became interested in geomancy, which is the art of seeing the earth as a sophisticated composition made up of different levels. These are the vital-energetic or etheric, and the emotional, spiritual and physical levels. After a few years I began to publish works on geomantic science. This is a modern kind of geomancy and my contributions would be rather incomplete if I were not working in a family team with my daughters Ajra and Ana. They are able to communicate with the universal consciousness which we used to call the angelic world. In this way my experience stemming from work in earth healing can be reinforced by a type of theoretical knowledge which does not depend primarily on any of the ancient traditions but rather is in tune with the steps of our future evolution.

One of the geomantic tools that I use in the places I have explored over the past 14 years is a careful observation of the radiation which emanates from the ground. As in the case of Sao Paulo, this can give one a good insight into the health or otherwise of a given ambience. All through those years I have observed again and again that the ground radiation conforms to one and the same pattern. The radiation stream emanates from the ground and flows straight upwards; and the height which it reaches is an accurate indicator of the life quality of the place.

Yet the radiation which streams from the ground also carries imprinted in it a kind of emotional quality which is an expression of the earth consciousness. During all those years I could feel that the quality of the ground radiation was impregnated with the will of the earth consciousness — we usually call it Gaia — which was to bring life into form, i.e., to materialize. Translated into the language of the four elements, earth, water, fire and air, this 'will to give form' corresponds to the element earth[3].

Yet during that night of the full moon on February 10th, 1998, when my intuition drove me out of my bed to test it, the ground radiation felt completely different. The vibration then did not follow the usual pattern which connected it to the earth element. Rather, I had the unmistakable feeling that the ground radiation had changed decisively. This time it was related to the element of water, and had a soft, watery and feminine character. The pattern began to form just above the earth, but then it did not continue in an upward direction but instead glided horizontally to and fro, as if someone was stroking a watery surface.

It remained like this for approximately one month, and was radically changed again on March 9th of the same year, this time to a rhythmic, fiery quality. Wherever I traveled, I could feel it. And there came yet another change during the night of April 19-20th. The quality now became like that of the air element, and adopted the characteristic spiral movement mentioned above in connection with the two faces of earth radiation found in the metropoli-

---

3 It may be confusing to refer to the four elements (water, fire, earth and air) when Chinese tradition speaks of five. One should remember that Chinese tradition is dealing with the five phases of the life process while the Western tradition is relating rather to the four basic qualities of the etheric world.

tan area of Sao Paulo.

Summarizing, I would say that during the time interval between February and April 1998 there was a decisive shift in the earth's etheric aura, and that this could be experienced through the changes in the ground radiation. These shifted through the whole spectrum, starting with the quality of the earth element, proceeding through the water and fire qualities, ultimately to reach the quality of the air element. Since then it has stayed the same, its fundamentals not changing any more. This means that the earth has woven for herself a new nest, or more precisely a womb, inside which she will successfully undertake her in-depth transmutation process during the coming age.

The symbolic meanings attached to the elements of earth and air may help us gain some better understanding of the transition of the earth's auric quality from one dominated by the element earth to one governed by the air element. I have mentioned already that the earth element stands for the processes which bring ideas into form and condense spiritual realities into matter. During the current era of earth's evolution, now apparently ending, it is obvious that the impulse to manifest in material form was given absolute priority.

The way we modern humans treat earth and nature mirrors the same tendency. We take them to be exclusively material objects which are fully perceptible through our physical senses and completely comprehensible by our mind.

In contrast, the quality of the air element represents something completely opposite. The symbolism of the air element stands for freedom, involving movement and communication between the different levels of existence. This means that through the inspiration of the air element, one should be able to move freely across the border that now sharply divides the materialized dimension of reality from its concomitant spiritual ones. In consequence, to deal with the emerging planet now governed by the air element, we will have to learn to perceive the invisible levels of reality as accurately as we perceive the material world today; even further, we will have to learn to move ourselves, with our consciousness and our bodies, through different dimensions of reality simultaneously; and also be able to be creative in conditions beyond the traditional split between spirit and matter.[4]

In the months following April 19-20th, 1998, when the last decisive change in the earth's etheric aura was completed, I had a hard time. On the one hand I was overwhelmed by the novel quality of the radiation that I could feel around me, while on the other I was constantly questioning how the earth changes would proceed and what would be the time rhythms of their manifestation. It was not that I had nothing to do, on the contrary I was busy traveling from country to country, working on my earth healing projects and giving talks and seminars. Yet the months were passing by while I remained in total uncertainty about how the process of the earth changes was progressing.

Nevertheless I knew deep inside me that the earth changes were continuing, but obviously on a level which my mind could not grasp and which were therefore incomprehensible to me. In that moment of great need I started to get clear and vivid dreams night after night, as if my inner self was trying to help me through the language of images.

For example, on August 31, 1998, I dreamed that I was a fisherman. While I was walking along the beach with my fishing rod, a gigantic fish appeared. Her head rose above the surface of the sea and she opened her mouth which was larger than a garage door. Her eyes, rather small but bright, were sparkling at me with unprecedented love. Instead of rejoicing, I started to worry, asking myself what I should do. As I was a fisherman, I thought, what else should I do but throw my fishhook into her open mouth? I felt the tiny hook travel down into the intestines of the giant fish, to be hooked at last in something soft. At that moment I realized the senselessness of my action.

The message of the dream touched me deeply, but it was not until months later, when the new phase of earth changes had become more transparent, that I could properly understand it. First of all, the dream was telling me that the new phase does not necessarily have to do with changes in power fields, but rather with the relationship between the living earth and the human

---

4 On the future role of the air element, see the 5th chapter of my book *Nature Spirits & Elemental Beings*, Findhorn Press 1996.

race. The giant fish represents the essence of the earth, her inner being, i.e., the soul aspect of the planet, which the ancients used to call 'Mother Earth' — in Greek, Gaia. There are a few traditions worldwide that depict her as a giant fish carrying the disc of the world on her back. In my own Slovenian folklore she is known as the 'Fish Faronika'[5]. She is responsible for the wellbeing of all life embarked upon her shoulders, and is able to provoke earthquakes and floods if the balances of life become disturbed.

The fisherman on the other hand represents the modern human being who is enamored of his excellent technology, which is based upon the exploitation of earth and nature. This technology is of course very disturbing to life as a whole and is symbolized in the dream by the fishing rod with its tiny hook, totally out of proportion relative to the immense power of the world soul and its manifold potentials.

These potentials are not recognized at all by our human culture, which concentrates on the material level of the earth and thus completely ignores the dimensions of its consciousness, its life forces and its spiritual essence. The message of the dream points to this new phase of the earth changes as being the moment when the earth starts to transcend her restriction to material form and opens her heart, pouring out her immense love towards all the forms of life embedded on her surface.

We have not noticed that radical changes are occurring in the conditions governing our existence upon this planet. Instead, our culture is automatically following its accustomed pattern of relating to the earth as to a material object, put at our disposal to meet our needs. Our failure to perceive the need for immediate changes in this pattern is a tragedy, and this was the main message of the dream.

In my meditations since May of 1998, I have also noticed that there has been a mutation in the earth's response to my attempts to approach it in its totality. Up till now, in order to be connected to the earth organism, it has been enough to connect through one's feet or go vertically down through the root chakra[g]. But not any more! Suddenly my intuition tells me that this has ceased to

---

5 On my experience of the Fish Faronika, see pages 20-22 of my book *Nature Spirits & Elemental Beings*.

be sufficient. To connect properly with the earth on the etheric, emotional and spiritual levels, one should bow one's head deeply down towards the ground and connect to the earth center through the crown chakra, as well as through the root center and the feet.

The experience of this way of making the connection has in turn introduced my consciousness to the sensation that the earth is no longer just under my feet but all around me. I started to relate to her as one does to the cosmos, whose dimensions spread all around one's being. Instead of calling her 'earth', I began to use the expression 'earth cosmos'. Only then did I become aware that there is a correspondence, even on the physical level, to this all-round approach which embraces earth from all sides. If one considers that the thick layer of air above us also belongs to the body of the earth — and this is correct even if it is not as dense as the geological strata — the earth does indeed spread all around us, and we are surrounded by it.

The sensation that I am no longer walking on earth's outer space, but participating instead in her inner space, and even standing within her being, has been simultaneously complemented by my perception of a very special kind of blue light which emanates from her core. I perceive it as being impregnated with an immense feeling of love, connecting me with her whole being in an unprecedented closeness. It is exactly the same feeling that I experienced shining through the loving eyes of the giant fish in my dream.

The next step towards understanding the significance of the new phase of earth changes was introduced to me in a dream on December 15th, 1998. It started with the presentiment that deep down in the cellar a waste water-pipe is leaking. So I go down the stairs to the cellar to discover that water is indeed gushing out of the concrete wall. Anticipating that I will have to break up the concrete and search for some fault in the plumbing, I give way to despair. But in the next moment I become aware that the water that is gushing from the wall is not sewage after all, but crystal clear spring water!

Before I can recover from my surprise, I see that around the corner there is an extension to the cellar, with cages forged from massive iron rods all neatly arranged along its walls. But now look! In one of them there is a fire igniting all by itself and starting to burn! I jump towards it and drag the cage to the middle of the cellar so that the fire will not damage the house.

I recognized immediately that these images were related to some strange events which had cropped up after May of 1998 and were challenging my understanding of what was going on. Just as in my dream my predominant thought had been that the leaking fluid must be sewage, so too these events seemed to suggest that there were negative, even destructive and unpleasant powers at work. And yet, looking with the inner eye, I realized that just opposite was true. They turned out to be incredibly pure and powerful. Let me give some examples.

At the beginning of May, 1998, a strong earthquake struck the western border of Slovenia, which is my country. Even though some villages were badly damaged, nobody had been hurt. Some friends who live there shared with me their feelings during the tremor. They sensed that the earth was taking great care not to create more damage than necessary. When I visited the place shortly afterwards and looked with my inner sight into the area's central mountain, called Krn, I realized that inside its belly new dimensions had manifested which I had not known before. I had the sense that the unpleasant quaking of the place's physical level was necessary to make space for something new, which has to be prepared for the future.

A few days later, on May 12th, I arrived at Sonnenhausen, a place near Munich in Germany where the Schweisfurth Foundation has its educational center. I was to hold one of my annual Earth Healing seminars there. When I went to look for sites where we could work with the seminar group on the following day, I visited a place in the nearby forest which is impregnated with the presence of elemental beings and nature spirits. I knew it very well from previous years, yet this time I was shocked. Not long before, a mighty beech tree had been broken by the wind in such a way that its crown was leaning against the neighboring trees, which continued to grow and flourish. The quality of the spiritual atmosphere around the tree was surprisingly high, and there was no trace of sorrow even though the destruction was obvious. When I attuned to the subtle levels, I saw a double vortex composed of a red power thread and a blue one ascending vertically out of the ground. My intuition whispered in my ear the notion that the tree had had to break up to make space for a new power source which needed to emerge on the earth's surface.

I found a few similar situations during the following months, always accompanied by the same kind of fresh and healthy power emanating from the ground. During the second half of 1998 I noticed that even my own life had adopted a similar pattern. There were nights when I could not sleep for a second; also, I had twisted my leg while working in Brazil; and I do not want to speak of the nasty colds which repeated themselves over and over. Yet in the midst of all these events, so personally disturbing, I was endowed with unexpected insights and inspirations.

After the New Year in 1999 the nature of the second phase of the earth changes became much clearer to me. By that time the process had advanced to the point that I could begin to perceive the 'new powers', without my being dependent on strange events breaking through the web of physical reality. Since that time they simply appear as round openings in the etheric organism of a place. Through these openings a new and unknown kind of power is emanating and spreading throughout the ambience.

The surprising characteristic of this power is that it can have both an earthly and a cosmic quality simultaneously. For example, my attention would be drawn down to the bottom of one of these power sources, and there perceive a kind of spinning dynamic taking place. But in the next moment I would become aware that the same underground earthly power was connected to the stars, and perceive it gliding over the cosmic sphere. In my geomantic work up till then, I had encountered all sorts of surprising phenomena, but all had one characteristic in common: their quality was either yin or yang and they either emanated from the earth or belonged to the cosmic realms. They could not be both at the same time! Yet obviously, the 'new power' is both.

Another striking peculiarity of these so-called 'new powers' is their variability. Even though they always display the same basic pattern described above, they appear each time in a different form. During the course of this year I have observed hundreds of them throughout different countries in Europe and America, and yet I have never come across two of them which are alike. They obviously have nothing to do with the mechanistic type of reality that we are used to. To mark this peculiarity I sometimes tend to call them 'new powers', and in other cases I use the singular 'new power' to denote that they represent one and the same archetypal force.

During my stay in Rio de Janeiro, Brazil, in August 1998 I visited a private home which also served as a cultural center under the name of the Vila Riso. This turned out to be one of the places which are strongly impregnated with this mysterious new power. For example, I was shown a spot in the garden where, during a tempest a month before, a huge tree had been literally blown out of the ground to fall precisely into the only vacant space between the buildings which stood all around. In the place where it had stood, I became aware of a double vortex emanating from the depths of the ground, similar to the one that I mentioned earlier in connection with my experience in Sonnenhausen in Germany. While there I had an exceptionally clear dream about the unusual nature of the 'new power'. In my dream I saw two persons, a woman and a man, who were lying naked in a hole in the ground in such a manner that they complemented each other like the black and white fields in the yin-yang sign. They themselves were mutates, which means a strange mixture of black and white. It was night, and yet I could see them as if by day. While they were lying in the ground their gaze was gliding across the heavenly sphere, ornamented with innumerable stars. There was somebody watching them constantly to make sure they did not fall asleep. And yet it was clear that they did go to sleep for ten minutes now and then, without their constant watching being disrupted.

Referring to the images in the dream, it is quite easy to recognize some of the above-mentioned characteristics of these 'new powers'. They do not conform to the usual order which places phenomena either at the feminine or the masculine poles, nor are they split between the earthly and cosmic levels. The main pattern of the dream emphasizes again and again their illogical nature. This allows them simultaneously to be both dark and light, feminine and masculine, yin and yang, asleep and awake, and belonging both to the earth and the heavens at the same time.

According to the language of the Bible, the 'new powers' which are appearing during this second phase of the earth changes can be identified as the primeval powers which governed the universe before the first day of creation dawned, that is before the separation of light from darkness. It is said that chaos prevailed before that first divine act which began the ordering of the universe. Yet today, through chaos research, we know that chaos does not refer simply to a state of disorder but to a primeval united force-field from which sprang all created things and all information.

One can very well understand what a healing effect such primeval powers can have upon a planet that has been utterly divided and restructured by human civilization. The general pattern of our behavior is to separate and govern by splitting apart the opposites that belong naturally together to form a whole. Obviously, our mind can only retain its rule in a world of dualities, where opposing forces weaken each other in constant battles. Thus disempowered and overstructured, the life-force can be used relatively efficiently to serve egocentric human needs. But in innumerable ways its functioning within the greater whole of the planetary organism is dramatically weakened and blocked. As a result ecological devastation starts to spread.

Obviously at the opposite pole to this pattern of human behavior, these 'new powers' which are right now spreading around the planet are powers that in their innermost nature deny any sort of separation. They stand for the primeval unity of the universal whole and are capable of restoring that unity wherever it has been broken and the powers of life dissipated. Their healing effects should be comforting and highly regenerative for the earth cosmos, but could be very unpleasant and disruptive for human civilization if we continue to resist any fundamental changes in our relationship to the earth as a biological, etheric, emotional and spiritual whole.

Going back for a moment to my dream of the leaking water-pipe, I should point out that in it I was given a vision of hope. I saw cages forged from massive iron rods, all neatly arranged along the cellar walls; they were hardened structures and as such represented the patterns of separation that human civilization is so stubbornly pursuing. Then I was shown how fresh fire could be ignited within them. One can very well imagine that the primeval powers which the earth is starting to manifest on her surface can act as the spark — even by using a subconscious pathway — to inspire people en masse to take courage, transcend the old patterns and once again fall in love with the cosmic whole.

Yet it would not be right to keep stressing the importance of these forgotten powers of universal unity, now reappearing on the earth's surface, without also pointing out that a far-reaching change is vibrating through the level of the planetary consciousness. Of course, I am not referring to consciousness only in the abstract sense of the word, but specifically to the nature spirits and elemental beings through whom the consciousness of the earth manifests itself to become aware of all the myriad of life processes encompassing the globe. If the consciousness of the earth were not to translate itself into the countless variety of etheric units which take care of different beings and life-forms — we usually call these etheric units either elemental beings or nature spirits — it could not properly direct and balance the ever-changing web of life.

In April 1999, when I was wandering through Amsterdam in Holland to prepare for my third Earth Healing workshop there, I found a group of 'new power' sources in Rembrandt Park. I was attracted to the possibility of showing them to the workshop group and so giving the participants the opportunity to experience their quality. But I also found several other places in the park where the presence of the new vibration could be strongly felt, but was manifesting itself in a completely different way.

One of those places was characterized by a strong white light within which I saw a multitude of white beings approaching the earth's surface in solemn procession. Another place built its momentum up from the very ground in the form of a spiral around which moved small etheric beings dressed in earthy and greenish colors. In this case too, it was obvious that the 'new powers' were present so that I could not simply identify it as a center of elemental beings, similar to those which I have known for years. There was a third place of this kind which could be described as balancing between the first two, for it was focussed on an exalted being of archetypal nature who gave the impression of standing on a cloud just above the ground, yet was stretching one leg out as if wanting to step down.

My sense was of meeting new types of etheric beings such as I had never encountered before. Is it possible, I wondered, that parallel to the upsurge of the 'new powers', new and previously unknown elemental beings are also manifesting within the invisible realms of the earth? Who are they? Are they representative of the archetypal layers of earth consciousness that belong to the sub-elemental world stored deep within Gaia's body?[6] Or do they belong to those famous extraterrestrials that for several decades now have challenged the materially oriented human mind?

To clarify these questions I needed to distance myself from my possible fantasies, so I asked my daughter Ajra Migka to refer them to her angel master who has for years been guiding her in her healing work. During the past few years the three of us have often worked together on earth healing projects, and at that time, in June 1999, we were at Findhorn, Scotland, conducting a week-long workshop dedicated to the recent earth changes and their impact on places, landscapes and the people inhabiting them. It was obviously the right moment to ask these questions.

First of all, the angel master rejected the idea that my observations might be dealing with a new kind of elemental being or nature spirit. He stressed that they belong to the existing beings who are embodying the earth consciousness. Those which, for example, I met in Amsterdam only seem to be different because they are undergoing a process of deep transmutation. This is why new, previously unknown qualities will start to speak through them. He called them 'obstetricians of the new earth'. Through the transmutation that they are undergoing, they are getting to know the directions which the earth changes will take, so that they will be able to offer effective help to the earth and its living organisms during the anticipated birthing process.

Referring to the above-mentioned beings who have been communicating their intention to step down to the earth, he said

---

6 For more on my experiences of the sub-elemental level of space, see my book *Healing the Heart of the Earth*, Findhorn Press 1998

that they belong to the servants of the air element. I did not recognize them as such, because they are embodying additional qualities needed in the process of change, of which the first is the quality of freedom. They would weave the quality of freedom into the elemental atmosphere of the earth, to be the basic quality of the emerging age.

Also, the angel master stressed that the primary task within the framework of the earth changes is the transmutation of elemental beings, since they have the abilities and competence to help the earth manifest her evolutionary path. Just as angelic beings are helping humans to grow spiritually, the elemental beings are helping the earth to unfold according to her intentions. The extraterrestrials, he added, have insufficient knowledge of the substance of the earth to be able to help the planet in such a complicated proceeding.

At the end of July, 1999, I happened to visit a place in my country, Slovenia, where I observed vast quantities of elemental beings filling the atmosphere with their bright presence. It seemed if they were all dressed in robes which were completely white, a sign of the renewal process they are going through. I asked them the simple question, what were they doing there. They instantly reacted by gliding apart to form a big circle around a piece of bare ground. I noticed then that through the surface features of the ground, I could recognize the blurred contours of a giant woman sleeping just below. At that moment the underground woman started to slowly move her arms and legs; then her face began to rise through the upper layer of the earth. I could see her beginning to open her eyes, perceiving the daylight for the first time after a sleep of ages..."The earth is going to awake to the full power of her presence, and we are preparing to help her become who she is in her totality," was the elementals' message. It is indeed inspiring to review the first steps in the process of earth changes and see with what rapidity the changes follow each other — but we should not expect the path to be without its dangers. There have been a few occasions during the two years 1998 and 1999 when I have been put on alert to be prepared for possible collapse. One should not forget that the earth has strayed from the secure path of development and is wandering along a knife's edge to reach a new level of safety.

What makes the situation more dramatic is the fact that humanity en masse is not supporting this hazardous undertaking, and is not even aware of the decisive turn that the earth's evolution is taking right now. On the contrary, modern civilization tends to oppose any in-depth change by simply denying the relevance of the levels of reality on which the evolutionary quantum leap is taking place.

On April 19th, 1999, before leaving Amsterdam, I had a dream. In it, I was sitting at my desk at home and as if by chance I looked out of the window. I was upset to see the landscape below our house leaning over to one side like a stranded shipwreck. The light was dim and had a poisonous quality. I was sure that the earth's axis was about to collapse. Jumping out of the house to test the ground radiation, I found it totally disjointed, displaying uneven movements, jerking and recoiling. I got in a panic and was about to call my wife so we could give first aid, but I had lost my voice and could not tell her what to do.

When I got out of my hotel in Amsterdam and tested the ground radiation with my hands, I discovered that its usual vibratory pattern was indeed seriously damaged. It took the two following days before the pattern was restored to its original rhythm and quality. In this context, it was not difficult to understand the dream as a warning that during the process of earth changes there could well arise sudden convulsions similar to the cardiac infarct which we know from our human experience. Its message made me realize the annihilating effect that panic stricken fear may have. This may be especially dangerous if it is experienced by millions of people who are quite unaware that the earth is walking a path of transmutation, and are oblivious to the possibility of an occasional partial collapse. Then, instead of helping her overcome the crisis, a wave of mass hysteria could cause the planet's final collapse.

To prevent such a hazardous reaction, it is important to broadcast the message that the earth changes are indeed taking place right now, although they are unfolding on an unexpected level where they are for the most part invisible. We should be grateful that the process can thus be accomplished in much safer and more peaceful ways than those predicted by the ancient seers. They foresaw that the changes would come through terrible wars and cataclysmic upheavals. Nostradamus was the best known among them and, writing in the 16th century, foretold that the dreaded breakdown would happen in the last half of 1999.

The ancient seers could not know that human evolution would by that time have reached such a level of maturity that we would become able to consciously parallel the earth changes by accomplishing them within the microcosms of our psyche and etheric bodies and spiritual worlds. So there is no need for the process of change to fall upon us all at once on the physical plane where its consequences would be most devastating. It has become possible to guide the course of the changes from the physical up to the subtle levels of existence, which is where they are busily progressing now as I wish to demonstrate in this review of earth changes. It follows that the changes should only start to manifest step by step on the physical level, which will make it possible for the earth to handle them in a much less disturbing way.

The input of human consciousness has an immense capacity to affect the form in which the earth changes take place, and this underlines our responsibility for them. This was first brought home to me when I read the messages about the earth changes which my daughter Ana Pogacnik received from the angelic world during the period from late 1997 to the beginning of 1999. They state that this is the first time that it may be possible to make the transition to a new level of evolution through a conscious collaboration between the earth, us human beings and the angelic world. Yet it is only possible to meet the challenge in this way if all three partners fulfill their roles in the process.

The messages also sound a strong note of warning, that the safety of the transition can be seriously endangered if we human beings continue to ignore the larger, indeed universal, scale on which the process is taking place and we remain interested only in our human affairs, closed tight behind the walls of our own little world.

To summarize, the messages are urging us to open our hearts, leave behind everything that is not essential to life, and focus on the step that must be taken now.

Chapter Two

Who Earth is, Who I am — Insights into the Emerging Geomancy

Let us assume that my account of earth's present changes is accurate. This would suggest that it will start to play a very important role in our lives. Then, of course, we will want to ask, who is this earth? The theme of the first chapter emphasizes that the earth is a cosmic being who, right now, is advancing with enormous strides to make manifest her hidden potentials. Yet humanity — or at least that part which has been affected by the influence of Western civilization — has lost the sense of the earth's sphere being anything more than a mere ball of matter rushing through universal space.

This dichotomy entails a dangerous contradiction, testifying that modern civilization may have lost most of its living contact with the earth's reality. But we are not ourselves obliged to submit to the materialistic point of view which governs society. We can listen to the knowledge of the Western geomantic tradition or even to the Eastern wisdom of feng-shui. But even these alternatives present problems. First, there are some rather deep differences between these two ancient ways of relating to the earth and its landscape. Their roots are based in two different philosophical concepts regarding who the earth is, and what is its relationship to human culture. Yet they have one thing in common — and this is the second problem — they both relate to the earth as it was before the start of the recent earth changes.

Clearly, there are two aspects to the current challenge. First, in order to secure humanity's links with our planetary home and avoid the need to move to another planet — would you like to move to Mars? — we have to get rid of our dominant patterns of behavior and listen carefully to the earth. Second, my observations suggest that the earth is in the process of becoming something essentially different from the earth we knew from past experience. This means that for the time being we should forget all the various kinds of traditional geomantic knowledge, and instead investigate the possibility of 'inventing' a new kind of geomancy in tune with the changing earth.

But before we embark on a journey to discover the, as yet, unknown dimensions of our planet in transformation, I should state clearly that it is not my intention to describe any well-defined structure of fixed geomantic knowledge. This would in no way correspond to the ever-changing earth now in transition. What I can rather give are insights into a long-term process, and explanations distilled from the experience I have gathered over the past two years while I have been in communication with the emerging earth cosmos.

I became especially interested in redefining our geomantic knowledge when it became obvious to me that the earth changes will not simply affect us on the physical plane by way of the prophesied cataclysms, but instead are taking a sophisticated path and 'dancing' through the subtle levels of reality. It became clear to me that the process of renewing and re-creating the earth's etheric, emotional and spiritual fabric will play a decisive role in ensuring that the transformation of the planet can follow a relatively non-violent path. This posed a question. If we lack all insight into the new conditions of the earth's planetary body now manifesting, how can we consciously collaborate with her changes and help her in her efforts to avoid the destruction of life on her surface?

I took courage, and during my annual retreat in September 1999 asked about the nature of the emerging earth. Each year I spend a treasured week with my family on a tiny island in the Adriatic sea and there I have the rare opportunity to talk with the consciousness of the earth. By this, I refer to my daily conversations with an advanced member of the community of elemental beings and nature spirits who resides at the top of a rounded hill beside which stands the island church. Even though elemental beings do not know the kind of individuality which we are honored to enjoy, some, in the advanced stages of their evolution, do develop a sense of personality. In my friend's case, his individual note relates to his role as a keeper of the wisdom of the earth and has even found its echo in a name which he himself has revealed to me. He is called Julius[1].

Since the consciousness of the earth operates on the emotional level, the language that one must master to understand its messages is a mingling of inner sensations composed of images, intuitions and emotional qualities. It takes time for the human mind to learn how to translate the rather unstructured flow of nature's language into the finite words that we use to communicate among ourselves. But once the pattern is grasped, my consciousness has no problem translating it clearly and comprehensively for my understanding.

What may still be a problem is the 'subjective' influence of the structuring mind upon the 'objective' quality of a message from an elemental being. Yet this is a general problem that confronts us the moment we step outside the 'world of objective fact' which has been artificially created and sustained by Western culture over the last two millennia; and which, due to the impact of modern civilization, has spread across the planet as a whole.

Life's reality simply does not know the objectivity which we would like to believe exists everywhere and which enables us to operate securely within the framework of our rational mind. My experience of working with the earth cosmos shows, beyond shadow of doubt, that behind each so-called objective phenomenon there is a subjective kind of consciousness at work. Or more precisely, the subjective and objective aspects of reality are inseparable and permeate each other. This means that for one's perceptions to be truly real, one should not cling exclusively to the so-called objective facts, but also open one's heart and listen carefully to the weavings of reality behind the tapestry of rationally provable features. The perception or communication will of course be colored by the subjective note of the parties involved. However, this 'subjective note', which our culture tends to disparage, can also be called a note of love, because it indicates the

---

1 Conversations with Julius are reported in *Nature Spirits & Elemental Beings*, *Healing the Heart of the Earth*, and *Christ Power and the Earth Goddess*.

mutual respect which the partners to the discourse have for each other, each allowing the other to view them in the mirror of their souls.

It was in the early morning of September 11th, 1999, that I began my conversation with Julius, my friend from the nature kingdom, about the inner order of the earth cosmos. During the previous few days I had been conferring with him about the recent cycle of earth changes. On this occasion he first started to impregnate my mind with the idea that, right now, there are two faces of reality in play. One face is the prevailing world paradigm, the one in which we are accustomed to live and which we as a culture believe we understand completely. We are proud to be the masters of its destiny. The other face is a mystery to us. It is submerged in our subconscious, and we would rather not know of its existence. We fear the disturbance that its possible emergence could trigger in our lives. But sooner or later we cannot avoid touching upon it, because it will be the dominant reality in the future.

But Julius also wanted to make another point. As a civilization we have chosen to live in a particular world-paradigm and we are convinced that on this we are the best authority. But even this is delusory. Pointing to his own authority as representative of the voice of nature, he insisted on his premise that the biological landscape could not sustain its life without the 'vibrational underground', i.e., a number of bio-energetic force-fields and other geomantic phenomena. They are of course ignored by the scientific knowledge in our prevailing paradigm, and yet they represent the basic precondition for life to move and breathe at all.

This is why, disregarding the prevailing culture of the rational mind, the natural instincts of people worldwide have inspired many to re-discover such techniques as dowsing, feng-shui and other forms of geomancy. Their efforts are working to counterbalance modern science's extremely one-sided focus on the physical surface of reality. Yet, as we know, these realms of knowledge have again and again been labeled 'fringe' and expelled from the patterns of our official thought system. Because they transcend the materialist framework which has been imposed on logic, they are inappropriately labeled 'esoteric'.

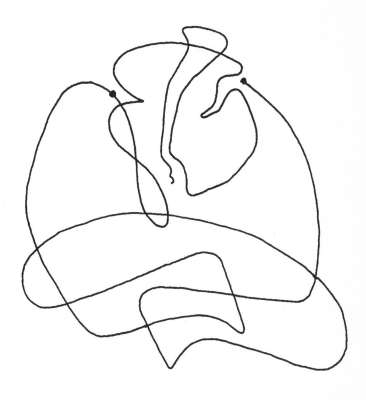

Julius, the old sage, my friend from the elemental world,
as he showed himself to me in August 1993
while I was preparing my book
Elemental Beings and Nature Spirits.

Julius was intent on impressing my consciousness with the idea that both sides, the publicly accepted and the publicly ignored, should be considered as equally important to the quality of life on earth. They belong together, and only by being linked to one another are they able to constitute the so-called 'five-dimensional reality' and make possible the forms of life as we know them today. Never mind what the human intellect may say!

At this point his communication took an exciting turn. Julius sees this five-dimensional reality as the one which will be transcended in the course of the present earth changes. By five-dimensional reality, I mean an ambience ruled by the three dimensions of physical space — width, height and depth; the fourth dimension is the time rhythm while the fifth could be called the 'bio-energetic' or 'etheric' dimension. This last is the one usually addressed by dowsers and geomancers.

Operating telepathically, Julius conveyed a rather peculiar picture which corresponded to this idea of coming transcendence. I saw this five-dimensional world structure like a rather stiff crust lying on the surface of the earth, while concealed beneath it were the various etheric organs and power centers that propel the life of the planet. Yet these existed submerged in a dim light similar to the world of dreams. But the power moving within the surface crust, representing life as we know it today, was of a nature a thousand times weaker than the power of the slumbering potentials of the earth beneath.

I realized that I had been shown the image of the earth in its present state. Yet the vision was imbued with a clear message that the world structure can no longer remain as it is. The planet has been pushed into such a divided state of being that it is losing its essential power and identity. This is one of the main reasons why it has moved onto the path of change. It is about to transcend the divisions inflicted on the earth cosmos by the temporary needs of human evolution.

The earth changes now about to happen may be presented as a three-fold process. First of all, we will witness a complicated process during which the five-dimensional crust, mentioned above, will break up and finally cease to exist as a separate layer of reality. Of course this will not be an easy experience for us humans, as we are accustomed to perceive it as the only kind of reality.

But even this does not mean that we will be facing a true cataclysm, such as some feared would strike us at the end of the second millennium. Why not? Because a parallel process is happening whereby the previously slumbering potentials of the earth will awaken to gradually manifest themselves in the immediate reality of everyday life. In this way, step-by-step, a new spatial structure will be constructed. In turn, this will offer the human race opportunities to adapt to the new conditions, and so stimulate us to take a forward step essential to our own evolution, and become closer to what we really are.

Mediating between the old and the new, we will witness a third process in which certain aspects of the five-dimensional ambience will become integrated into the new scheme of the earth cosmos. These are aspects that have some relationship to the reality of life and do not just express human arbitrariness. Especially, Julius meant the aspect that enables life to express itself through matter, i.e., to materialize. This quality should by no means be lost because it represents the unique contribution that the earth is able to offer to the universal whole.

After I had to some degree understood how the new reality of the earth was to manifest, I became interested in those of earth's geomantic systems that had been shown me as currently slumbering potentials. They are about to become the leading powers of the emerging earth cosmos and will obviously be the determining factors in the life conditions of our tomorrow, a tomorrow that is in some ways already 'today'.

It waswhen I received a strange dream in May 1998 that I had my first inkling that there exists a geomantic system of which I was ignorant. This was only a month after the completion of the first phase of the earth changes. I dreamt that I was walking through a forest and had arrived at the edge of a large clearing. To my surprise I saw a tiger there, basking in the hot rays of the sun. In order to sunbathe more completely, the tiger had divided itself into pieces, each of them separately exposed to the sun's rays. Noticing my presence, the beast instantly drew its parts together and disappeared into the jungle. Yet in its haste, the tiger forgot one of its majestic paws and left it in the meadow! I found myself pondering the possibility that I could take the paw, bury it beneath the earth, and so cripple the tiger forever.

The message of the dream remained a total mystery till a few months later when I started to experience a dimension of reality of which previously I had been unaware. It had been hidden deep within the subconscious realms of original space. But as the dream pointed out, this dimension must be of great importance to the mobility of earth's geomantic systems. What could a tiger do with only three legs?

These experiences occurred at the beginning of 1999 when I started to perceive power sources that I had never met before, as described in the previous chapter. As I said there, I am in the habit of calling these emanating powers 'new powers', because their characteristics are quite different from any of the geomantic powers I had met previously. They do not know any division, they can be simultaneously of an earthly and a cosmic quality, of a yin and yang nature, etc. They operate beyond the rationalizations of linear logic.

One could describe the geomantic system symbolized by the tiger's missing fourth leg as the basis for all the expressions of life. It relates to the deepest level of existence, that which nourishes all levels of life, visible and non-visible. Following an inspiration imparted by the angelic world, my daughter Ana started to call it the 'nourishing system of the earth'[2].

This inspiration was received on the 10th of February, 1999, when she asked the Angel of Earth Healing for insights to prepare me for an earth healing project at Dachau, a small town in the south of Germany . The place is known worldwide because of its extremely unfortunate history, having been the site of an infamous Nazi concentration camp during the second world war. I was planning to go there a month later to work with a group of 50 German people and seek to release the patterns that history had imprinted upon this geomantically very exquisite spot, and revitalize some of its power points.

---

2 I use the traditional term 'angelic world' to denote the universal (divine) consciousness which permeates the whole universe.

When Ana asked the angelic world for guidance on preparing the work correctly, it turned out that Dachau is in fact the location of the most powerful and prolific sources of the earth's nourishing system. In this transmission the Angel of Earth Healing described the system as the one which secured and nourished life in all its diverse facets. He portrayed the basic 'nourishing system of the earth' as being imbued with heart quality and composed of a number of sources which differ in their energy characteristics, yet are held together by a common vibration.

As mentioned previously, ever since January 1999 I have perceived the emergence everywhere of groups of sources belonging to the nourishing system of the earth — I cannot speak for the continents which I did not visit this year, but certainly this is true for Europe, and also parts of both Americas. This would mean that the earth is now activating her basic power sources and enormously accelerating her vibrations, so propelling all levels of her life to greater speed.

Together with the group that had gathered for the earth healing work, we visited a few of the main sources of the earth's nourishing system. They were located in and around Dachau over an area of about 18 kilometers (11 miles) diameter. Most of them were blocked by the destructive patterns projected upon the place during its oppression by the concentration camp and the accompanying emotional traumas. During the extremely difficult earth healing work[3] that we had to endure there, I got the notion that the Nazis knew the secret of the fundamental power system of the earth and had decided to locate the camp there, with the intention either of suppressing the power sources or even experimenting with their potentials. The Nazi regime might have known that these powers could be used for unprecedented destruction, as was revealed later by the explosion of the Hiroshima atomic bomb.

Only after I had got to know the nourishing system of the earth did I start to understand the symbolic meaning of the 'dragon'. The myths of traditional cultures all over the world tell of such tremendously powerful creatures. They belong to the realms

---

3 See the detailed description of my earth healing methods in my book *Healing the Heart of the Earth*.

of the deep earth or to the immense ocean depths, and only there is their atomic power kept properly enclosed and silenced by the cosmic order of the earth, which allots them a place where their presence and activity can be useful.

If they were to appear on the earth's surface, their presence would have devastating effects. Their image would then be associated with the destructive heat of fire, spreading death among living beings. In the myths, they are depicted as merciless monsters that do not know the gentleness of the heart. They would often appear out of a cave leading up from the underworld and demand the delivery of the kingdom's most beautiful women to be their food, so that the people might avoid the total destruction of the country.

In November 1999 I visited the United Nations building in New York with my daughter Ana, and there had the opportunity to experience the radiation from some everyday objects which had been exposed to the explosion of the atomic bomb in Hiroshima. The UN has put them on display to warn us against misusing atomic power to destroy life. I have never felt such a merciless presence of death as radiates from those objects.

My intuition instantly connected them with the myths which tell of the dangers of contacting the 'dragon powers' on the wrong level of existence. We, through modern atomic technology, are misusing the basic powers of earth. The powers of the nourishing system of the earth should manifest in a natural way, ascending through the different dimensions of reality to ultimately emerge as the internal power of life within living beings. Instead they are being stolen by a clever rationalism which invades the very basis of creation. The consequences are devastating, as we know from accidents at atomic plants and, of course, from Hiroshima.

The powers of the nourishing system of the earth should be properly balanced and contained in the place allotted them by nature. To emphasize this point, the ancient mythologies present us with the figure of the 'dragon slayer'. His spiritual task is not to kill the dragon — do not confuse symbolic images with reality — but to keep the dragon power in its proper place within the cosmos. In the West, one example is the image of the Archangel

Michael who is often portrayed in medieval sculpture, gently holding his spear deep in the open mouth of a dragon which lies beneath his feet. Life can only flourish if a proper relationship is maintained between the spiritual powers of the universe and the 'dragon powers' of the earth.

We found this same balance during our visit to the United Nations building on the East River. It contains not only the above-mentioned traces of the modern misuse of the 'dragon powers', but also the strongest focus of the spiritual forces of the universe that we had ever met. This focus is in a small meditation chamber created by Dag Hamersköld, one of the early Secretaries General of the UN. It offers delegates and visitors — for it is open to the public — the opportunity to express their religious needs without distinction of creed. Only one object is placed in the cone-shaped room, an altar-like meteorite of cosmic iron that fell from the starry sky in Sweden. I perceived a tremendous column of white light which pierced the ferrous stone and, imbued with unprecedented heart power, shone out to the world around. I believe that this power is working through the spirit of the United Nations to counterbalance the threat to the life of the earth posed by our civilization's misuse of the fundamental powers of life.

Traditional geomancy points out not only the dangers of the misuse of the nourishing system of the earth, but also describes how the 'dragon powers' have manifested creatively on the earth's surface since the beginning of time. It points to the so-called 'dragon paths' along which the dragons move secretly across the landscape. They leave behind them a trail of their life-nourishing powers to be absorbed by the living beings of the related ambiance, humans included.

When I use my inner sight to look at such a 'dragon path', I see an organically shaped stream of fiery energy very much like an invisible stream of volcanic lava. It stays close to the ground and floats along with a slow and majestic rhythm. I would describe its function as a stream of the sexual force of nature, which fertilizes all aspects of its kingdom. In pre-Christian times, pilgrim paths were often laid along these lines of the earth's sexual force to celebrate its creative powers. This tradition was still followed in the early Middle Ages when churches were frequently sited along

*The power stream of a 'dragon path' (below)
compared with the energy path of a ley-line (above).*

such 'dragon paths' to ensure a proper balance between the sexual powers of the earth and the spiritual powers of the universe. Such churches are often consecrated to the balancing power of the Archangel Michael.

To clarify this all-important point, let me repeat that during the past era of the planet's history the dragon-related phenomena have been linked to the relationship between the surface of the earth and its fundamental nourishing system; also, that the same life-sustaining system has recently started to manifest all over the earth in a new way. This has taken the form of clusters of power sources, from which its forces are emanating to gradually imbue the whole of earth's ambience with their unimaginably potent healing and life-empowering qualities.

Since, as human beings, we are fractals of the earth cosmos, anything that belongs to the essence of the earth must also find its expression in our human body/soul. So it should be possible to find something which corresponds to the nourishing system of the earth within the micro-systems which keep our being alive. A dream that I received on January 29th, 1999, showed me the way to search for its traces.

The dream went like this. I was visiting our workplace with my young woman assistant when someone approached her to offer her a necklace with a beautiful cosmogram engraved on a metal plate. My assistant behaved as if she had no interest in buying the precious article. However, I noticed that she liked it a lot, but thought she probably didn't have enough money. I decided to be generous and asked her if I might buy it for her. Then I put my hand in my back pocket where we men usually keep our wallets, drew it out and opened it proudly. To my disappointment, there were only two dollars in the purse...

Since the necklace's cosmogram would be placed over the wearer's thought chakra[g], I think it represents the creative abilities of the human being. The wallet on the other hand, positioned at the root chakra on the back of the body, denotes the basic nourishing powers that feed our chakra system with fresh archetypal forces.

The dream's message was that the 'shadow system' at our back — even if we don't pay any attention to it — is a prerequisite for the 'sunny side' of our being to function as we would wish, expressing itself in our creative activities.

Yet the message sounded a clear note concerning our future, which is coming closer through the process of the earth changes. It warns that it may no longer be possible for us to let 'the nourishing system of the back' slip into oblivion and operate exclusively from the surface of the cherished front side of our body's power system. In 1999, the earth opened her surface organism to the above-mentioned 'new powers' which emanate from her fundamental nourishing system, and just so we too should learn to lead the 'powers of the back' through our body to the front.

Seen in terms of the emerging future, one can imagine that the human force-fields will be enormously accelerated through the manifestation of archetypal powers that were previously stored in the depths of the earth. We should learn, step by step, to integrate the nourishing powers of our back into the wholeness of our life-sustaining systems. In this way we will become strong enough to exist in the conditions of the future earth and not get lost, victims of her enormously increased power and beauty.

The undifferentiated stream of the nourishing forces from our back feeds the manifold activities of our 'front chakras', just as the powers of the nourishing system of the earth feed the vital-energy organs of the landscape. In any given environment, these 'organs' perform their various functions which are similar to the 'front chakras' of the human body positioned along the spine. Just as we have there a heart center, solar plexus and root center, so does the landscape. I call these kinds of centers 'vital-energy organs', because they distribute vital powers throughout the landscape.

Within the holon[g] of each place, for example, one can find the vital-energy center which corresponds to the solar plexus of the human body. This center is responsible for permeating the landscape with vital powers. Usually, it looks like an etheric pump which constantly draws vital powers from the veins of the nourishing system located in earth's depths and adjusts them to the life-manifesting surface. In the last phase of the process, the vital-energy center spills them out radially into its environment to feed the life of the locality.

There is another kind of earth chakra which works through a pair of etheric centers. It represents the respiration system. One of the centers functions as the in-breath, the other, its counterpart, as the out-breath. The in-breath center takes the forces of its cosmic environment into the earth's depths. These cosmic forces will be adjusted within the belly of the earth to conform to the vibrational level of planetary life, and ultimately exhaled through the out-breath center to support the life processes of earth. We could call this the 'throat chakra' of a given environment.

The heart center is another kind of earth chakra that must be present in any holon. Its function is to revitalize the life forces of the environment and constantly imbue them with the love vibration of Mother Earth, which is a quality that life cannot dismiss without peril. The heart center continually draws in the forces of the environment, renews them and sends them out again.

There are also earth centers which function similarly to our crown chakra and connect the planet to different cosmic sources. They usually look like pillars of light linking earth's body to some extraterrestrial source of power and information.

Within each holon there is usually a system of yin-yang centers that correspond to our sexual chakra. Like the respiration centers, they operate as a pair and comprise separate yin and yang centers from which stream out, respectively, negative- and positive-polarized forces. There are many processes in nature and within human beings that need to be fed with polarized powers if they are to develop their creative momentum. The yin and yang centers of a specific environment are always in some way linked with one another, and their activity is balanced by the help of a third center which has a neutral quality.

I should also mention the grounding centers of a landscape. These correspond to our root chakra. The function of such centers is to prevent the subtle levels of a given ambience from drifting upwards and so losing their proper connection with the sources of the vital powers we have been describing, which are the planet's fundamental nourishing system. The etheric form of

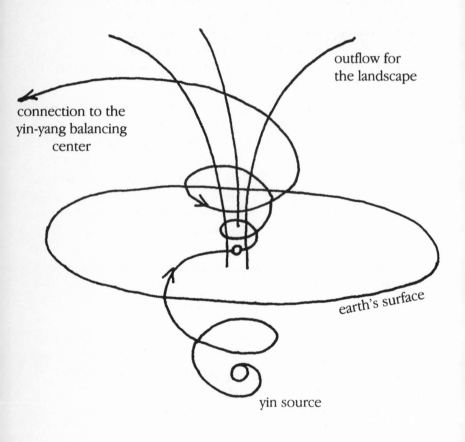

outflow for
the landscape

connection to the
yin-yang balancing
center

earth's surface

yin source

*An example of a Yin-Center
observed at San Pietro di Castello in Venice, Italy.*

a grounding center usually resembles a tree. Its branches connect to all of the landscape's multi-layered aspects, and its roots go deep down into the earth's body to anchor those layers firmly[4].

The purpose of this book is not to describe earth's glorious etheric garments in all their different aspects, but I do have to mention at least one other type of etheric planetary organ. This one is not structured around a center as are the chakras, but extends through the landscape in linear fashion. They are commonly called 'ley-lines', though one should be aware that a landscape contains a number of different linear phenomena which could also be called 'leys'.

In the context of the life-giving organs of the earth, 'ley-lines' do not mean lines denoting alignments between historical sites. Those belong to the cultural layers in the landscape and not to its nature organism. I am referring here to the true power ley-lines, which distribute the life forces throughout the etheric organism of a landscape, similar to the way acupuncture meridians distribute them within the human organism. Seen in my inner vision, a power ley-line appears as a dynamic composition of spiraling life force, piercing through the ambience of a given landscape in a straight but slightly undulating line. Imagine a fiery snake rolling through the landscape in great majesty, coiling uphill up and down, and always following a straight path which may cover a distance of many thousand miles.

There is a fascination in the endless variability and precise functioning of the power organs of the earth. Nevertheless, we are interested here not in details but in the wholeness of the earth cosmos, and so should carry on with our exploration. The next step is to give our attention to the planetary consciousness. It is an equally important and not less complex counterpart of the power organism of the planet.

These observations are all connected to my conversation with Julius, my friend from the elemental world, which I began to relate near the start of this chapter. I now decided to change the subject of the conversation and started to project a stream of emotions towards him, all loaded with my burning interest in the

---

4 One can find more information on vital-energy organs (chakras) in my book *Healing the Heart of the Earth*.

present state of the earth consciousness, and the role of elemental beings and nature spirits within its whole.

His answer was immediate and straightforward: "Elemental beings are the consciousness of the earth and have the task of conducting the impulses of the earth's soul from within the planet to its surface." The accompanying image showed elemental beings as forming a highly sensitive informational membrane wound all around the earth's sphere, and interacting with all the forms of life and phenomena which inhabit the planet's surface. This membrane is built up from countless numbers of smaller and bigger units, which we are accustomed to call elemental beings.

In effect there are two main layers of earth consciousness in play. The deepest layer could be called the 'earth soul'. It is composed of a certain number of powerful archetypes who represent the planet's identity. In the first chapter of my book Nature Spirits and Elemental Beings, I describe my experience of some aspects of the earth soul. I met them after going outside of my daily awareness through a 'dark tunnel' deep down into what I call the 'sub-elemental world'[5]. This could be compared to those layers of our own subconscious where the collective archetypes of humanity are stored. These archetypes represent the 'underground' in which are rooted our human identity and inspirations for cultural creativity.

In the course of my earth healing work I have had the good fortune to get to know some of nature's sacred places. These represent a kind of opening in the consciousness of the earth, through which it is possible to approach the earth soul. One of them is located in the midst of the Black Forest in south-west Germany. It takes the form of a rather small but perfectly round and extremely deep lake which lies quiet and still at the foot of a mountain that I came to know as a sanctuary of the earth soul. The mountain's name is Hornisgrinde.

When with awakened consciousness I went through the lake into that dark tunnel and arrived at its lower end, I found myself walking — or rather floating — through a landscape inhabited by

---

5 See also the chapter on the sub-elemental level of space in *Healing the Heart of the Earth*, pages 111-119.

plants. There was no animal or human being to be met there but only plants of fantastic shapes and beauty. The beauty was so powerful and pristine that it nearly took my breath away. It is the paradise lost, or better put, retired, and carefully protected within the depths of the earth soul.

If the sub-elemental level of the earth soul can be compared to the human subconscious, then elemental beings — or 'nature spirits' as some call them — represent the consciousness of the earth cosmos. It is this vast consciousness, composed of all kinds of elemental beings, which actively participates in the whole variety of life operations upon the planet. They represent the fully awakened and active aspect of the Mother Earth.

Julius, my friend from the nature kingdom, continued, "It is not by chance that human beings have become the companions of the earth planet. It is because you are following a similar evolutionary path." Pointing to our ability to think independently and to be free in our creativity, he went on, "Also, the earth differs from some other planets in having developed its own consciousness, which manifests through the world of elemental beings. Of course too, there is the angelic intelligence that permeates the whole universe. It also interacts with the earth consciousness, yet respects its autonomy." His words indicate that on earth there are three strands of evolution related to the planet's consciousness; they are to a high degree self-conscious and autonomous and yet are involved in a common purpose: they are the angelic, the human and the elemental.

Seen in this way, the elemental beings do not just embody the unified field of earth's intelligence, but also represent a specific evolution, similar to that of the plants, animals and human beings. There is of course one obvious distinction. The beings belonging to the animal, human and plant evolutions can be easily perceived by our physical senses and studied through the tools of the rational mind. This is not the case with the beings of the elemental evolution. Here we have to deal with beings who do indeed have a body, but not one condensed in a physical form. Rather, their bodies are composed of etheric vortexes and fields of life-power, so that they appear close to formless.

The spirit of coton
as seen by the Mesoamerican culture of Paracas.

This does not mean that they do not have a practical role in life. On the contrary! The different kinds of elemental beings have roles that can be compared to the various tasks performed by the different parts of our brain: supervising the proper functioning of body organs; reading and interpreting the messages collected by our nervous system; storing memories etc. The elemental beings have to perform all these various functions, not only in relation to the earth as a whole, but also for each separate plant — whether it is a tiny blade of grass or a gigantic tree — and also for the other living beings that walk upon the earth, such as animals and even individual humans.

To permit the performance of such a rich variety of tasks, the evolution of elemental beings is known for its extreme diversity. Basically, their evolution comprises four main streams, each related to the scheme of the four elements. There are beings who serve and grow through the Element of Water, which means that they have to do with the life streams. There are others who belong to the Element of Air and deal with all the different kinds of interactions and processes which go on in a given ambience. Those whose main characteristic is to follow the Element of Earth work with the processes of manifestation and materialization of forms. The beings of the Fire Element supervise the processes of change, of death and rebirth.

I was lucky enough to get some clear answers to my questions about their different kinds of roles while I was exploring a center of elemental beings on Meissner Mountain, near Kassel, Germany. A volcano shaped it in ancient times, and according to tradition it is a sacred mountain dedicated to the Goddess named Lady Holle or Hella. The place where I discovered the center of elemental beings is located at the edge of a plateau and is known as Kitzkammer.

While I was sitting beside the nearby stream and attuning to the elemental beings of the water — traditionally known as nixies — they unexpectedly started, in their emotional language, to talk about the work they perform. "The water of the stream is rich with liquid ether, which is the gift it receives from the Mother Earth. We combine it with the air element from the surrounding atmosphere and with the fire ethers taken from the solar rays. We are working ceaselessly to interlace these three elements into braids that spread out into the environment to imbue it with the quality of life eternal."

To show to me the 'technology' they use, they pointed to my knees — I was seated on the bank of the stream — and in an instant made them yin-yang polarized. They commented, "When we interlace the life quality, we use the natural polarization of stones and banks as our tool." And in the same moment they manifested a spinning wheel of fire ethers interacting with a cloud of watery aura between my polarized knees.

When I moved a bit higher up, to the foot of a basalt rock which jutted proudly above the stream, I became aware of fire spirits moving rhythmically within the volcanic stone. Having just had the enlightening experience with the water beings, I took my courage in both hands, so to speak, and asked them to demonstrate, on my own body, the service they perform for the earth soul. To my surprise, they appeared to catch me rather violently under my arms. For a moment I thought that it would be safer to resist what they were doing, but instantly decided to hold to my decision and be open to them. So they catapulted me high into the atmosphere. The higher I flew through the air, the less densely material I became, until ultimately I was pure vibration only.

Their message was clear. They work to decompose all kinds of material forms when their purpose is finished, and to guide the powers 'frozen' in the form back to the original ocean of vibration. But do not dare call them harbingers of death! The elemental beings of fire consider themselves to be harbingers of freedom — and that is what they are.

Both the above instances concern one center of elemental beings, who are simply performing their role as a fractal of the consciousness of the earth. Each landscape is crisscrossed with such centers. But there are also mega-centers, though these are very rare. They perform a highly specialized task, usually for the whole of a given landscape or for a vast portion of a country. For example, there is a special center of elemental beings in Sarajevo, Bosnia. The Angel of Earth Healing showed this to my daughter Ana while we were preparing an earth healing project for the city, very much damaged during the civil war of a few years ago. The center is located at the edge of a Moslem cemetery, on a hill called Cicin Han.

Dimension	Geomantic manifestation	Correspondence within the human being
Nourishing system of the Earth	sources of archetypal powers	archetypal powers of the back
	"dragon power"	sexual power
Vital-energy dimension	vital-energy organs (power centers)	system of chakras
	ley-lines (energy paths)	acupuncture meridians
Planetary consciousness	sub-elemental level (archetypes of the Earth)	subsonsciousness
	elemental beings and nature spirits	emotional level of consciousness
	self-consciousness of the Earth (Gaia)	mental consciousness

The geomantic dimensions of the Earth

In July 1999 we were working there with an international group of enthusiasts to wipe out the traumas of the war. I perceived the center then as a huge sphere located just beneath the ground. It is composed of innumerable, differently colored facets, and its interior is structured with conical ventricles. The elemental beings were operating there like bees, constantly going in and out and spreading out through the landscape. My insight told me that they were distributing impulses essential for the fecundity of the land.

Returning to my discourse with Julius, keeper of earth knowledge, I now expressed my wish to know more about the evolution of elemental beings. By way of answer, he triggered in me the thought that their development knows different phases, as is the case with the human evolutionary path. First, he referred to the challenges that faced the evolution of elemental beings millennia ago, at the dawn of the present age, when "the earth had to fundamentally reshape its spatial dimensions so as to become an appropriate workshop for human beings to develop their sense of freedom and personal autonomy." In that phase they had, together with other subtle dimensions of the earth, to disappear from the visible world and learn something completely new: to govern life 'from behind the scenes' and to sustain the so-called five-dimensional reality (i.e., the materialized world) which we needed in order to develop. Only in the harsh conditions of an earth known as 'the vale of tears'[6], could we learn to be creative out of our own center and to love out of our own heart, without being constantly dependent on guidance from the universal whole.

This is why, for millennium after millennium, elemental beings have had to support a landscape characterized by the physical rigidity of matter. It can be depicted as a dense tapestry or sort of stage-prop scenery, behind which was hidden the multidimensionality of the earth.

The present era of earth changes is initiating a radical turnabout in the evolution of the elemental beings, who are now facing a new and different kind of challenge. They are having to learn how to introduce all the subtle dimensions of the earth cosmos of which we spoke above into a world that in the meantime has become a physical reality.

---

6 The harsh conditions of the world where Adam and Eve had to settle after they had been, according to the Bible, 'expelled from Paradise' are another appropriate image.

Chapter Three

How to Perceive
the Invisible Side of Reality

At this point I am going to rest my presentation of the different dimensions of the 'new' reality. There is little sense in talking about all the interesting phenomena inherent in the earth cosmos if the reader does not have personal experience of their immediate presence. Then it remains all abstract knowledge that is of little use if you cannot prove it for yourself through your own emotional, intuitive, mental or even bodily experience. Theories can be splendid. But as long as we do not experience them as relating to our everyday life, they are not of much value to us.

The human being is a free being. Freedom is the divine gift that is our birthright. It constitutes our identity as human beings, and consequently it is wrong for us to blindly give our trust to anything or anyone, even if the arguments advanced are absolutely convincing. In order to trust and support someone else's ideas and concepts, we should secretly listen to our heart — our inner sensations or intuitions — and decide 'in the moment' whether the path being advocated corresponds to the basic principles inscribed within our heart's core.

Yet I must emphasize that I do not wish to reinforce an attitude of doubt, which is a tendency the rational mind has implanted in human consciousness during this era of its dominance. If we nurture our doubts, we close our hearts and awareness to those expressions of life which are too challenging or too beautiful to be accepted within the mental and emotional patterns of the governing culture and mass media, which we have allowed ourselves to adopt.

When I teach the perception of invisible reality in my work-shops, I have noticed time and again that people use their doubts to 'kill' their perceptions. They do so because their mind is afraid it will lose control of their experiences. We are taught to doubt an 'unorthodox' experience at the very moment it surfaces in our consciousness. A subtle perception can be destroyed as soon as it appears at the gate of our awareness. It is enough for the usual psychic pattern to come into play and exclaim — even for a split second — "I am not sensitive enough to have such a beautiful perception." What follows is an immediate blackout.

Instead of doubting, one should learn to trust ceaselessly. I do not mean trusting somebody else's ideas and preconceptions, but trusting oneself. It means trusting that human beings are pre-destined to naturally perceive all the levels and dimensions of reality around us, simply because we are an integral part of those levels and dimensions. We should ask ourselves how, since they are within us, could we possibly not perceive them if they appeared around us?

We do not need to develop some special sensitivity in order to enjoy the presence of elemental beings. We just need to accept the natural stream of incoming information and let it find its prop-er expression within our consciousness. We should not allow our ingrown mechanism of doubt to stop it before it can even reach our awareness!

This brings us to the first principle to be considered in order for us to open ourselves to holistic perception:

1. Replace Your Patterns of Doubt with Patterns of Trust

You should know that the ability to perceive visible and invisible levels of reality is the most natural ability we have. Work on yourself persistently, so as to recognize and transmute your patterns of doubt. Do not allow your own rational mind to rob you of the most delightful insights into the beauty of life, thus holding you constantly imprisoned within the cage of the cultural preconceptions that she has adopted. Instead, we should all learn to trust continuously.

Replacing doubts with trust does not mean that we should

stop being self-critical. On the contrary! It is important that the mind should maintain a proper distance even while it accompanies the stream of our perceptions. It should watch us to make sure we are properly grounded and attuned to what we are perceiving. It can warn us if our imaginations go too far and we lose ourselves in fantasies. It can make us aware if we push beyond the boundaries of the possible. Allow your mind to make her comments from a safe place 'aside', but do not allow her to break into your perceptions and destroy them before they are even born.

Consequently, the next step in the preparation for holistic perception is to:

2. Work on Transcending Mind Control

Be aware that in the course of our culture's modern development we have given our own rational mind the permission to completely control our perceptions. It follows that at each moment the minds of billions of people are — mainly subconsciously — deciding, out of the diversity of phenomena perceived, which ones correspond to our civilization's preconception of reality, and which ones do not. Those which do are allowed to appear in our consciousness, and those which don't are *wiped out mercilessly*.

So, if you trust your perceptions and you are still perceiving nothing beyond what is usual for this culture, you should know that your own mind control is deleting your perceptions. You yourself are robbing yourself of the experiences that you yourself wish to have. For how much longer are you prepared to tolerate and suffer under this stupid contradiction?

I like to tell the story of Jesus the Christ's comments on the problem of the mercilessness of mind control. He was born into the era when the rational mind was starting to take over the dominant position in the human consciousness, and he was of course aware of the damage that its unreflective rule could inflict upon the wholeness of the human being[1]. In the

1 For more on the Christ's words concerning the theme of mind control, see my book *Christ Power and the Earth Goddess*, pages 112-119 and page 251.

words of the Bible, "If the householder knew at what time the thief would come, he would not let anyone break into his house." (Luke 12:39)

Within the framework of a culture ruled by reason, the householder stands for the controlling mind and the thief for the perceptions, intuitions and experiences that are usually suppressed by the patterns of reason. The words of Jesus require us to listen to the message we are prone to dismiss, the message of those perceptions, intuitions and experiences which, like a burglar, can surface in an unexpected moment to outsmart the mind's total control over our consciousness. Do not identify with the 'householder' and devote yourself fully to him! See how you can help your 'thief' successfully break into your house again and again!

3. Accept the Fact that You are Co-Creating Your Perceptions

In the last chapter I stated my premise that life (i.e., nature, the earth) does not know the kind of objectivity which people want to see existing everywhere around them, so that their rational mind can feel fully secure as it operates in the world. Information pulsates from all levels of our environment — the physical level included — and its messages reach our perceptive organs as *pure light impulses*. It is our consciousness that always finds a way to read those impulses, creating appropriate images and concepts so that the message becomes understandable to the mind.

For example, in the split second that we look at a chair, we just don't notice what a complicated process is running through us to enable us to recognize it as a chair. Yet we should be aware that the same process goes on with no less intensity when we 'look' at a nature spirit and try to figure out what role it plays within the fabric of a landscape.

The circumstances in which we were born make the only difference between the two kinds of process: the fact that our culture has imprinted upon our consciousness some very decisive, even pedantic, rules and patterns which make it quite easy to recognize a chair as a chair; but to perceive a nature spirit, the situation is just the opposite. The ruling rational mind doesn't even accept the fact that such a phenomenon can exist, so it can offer no patterns to ensure that the nature spirit can always be recognized for what it is. If our perception were to depend only on the mind's decision – and this is the case with most of modern mankind – the only possible answer our consciousness could give would be that the poor nature spirit does not exist at all.

Yet the traditions of fairy-tales and the artworks created in past times provide a wealth of testimony that various ancient cultures could create their own language which gave nature spirits the space to express themselves through the consciousness of the culture's members. They invented ways, in initiations and teachings, to hand down those patterns of perception from generation to generation, in order to secure a common understanding of what people perceived within the earth cosmos.

I'd like to share some experiences of the way elemental beings appear in different forms relating to the cultural pattern of the respective country involved. Working in Europe on my book Nature Spirits and Elemental Beings, I was often surprised to see them as they are presented in the books of children's fairy-tales. In this case, as I understood later, I was subconsciously relating to the medieval fairy-tale tradition, the only one that Europeans have kept alive throughout the later rationalist centuries — though of course not for adult reading, but to entertain their children.

Arriving in Brazil and later in Mexico, I was no less surprised to see nature spirits in the forms characteristic of the artwork of the ancient Indian cultures, Toltec, Mayan, etc. My mind had problems in making this switch. My intuition, on the contrary, accepted the difference immediately. The elemental beings had obviously adopted the 'language' of their communication with the respective indigenous cultures during the previous centuries. Because the white people who ruled there later did not relate to them at all, the nature spirits had no opportunity to learn the European pattern of 'language'. This is the reason why my consciousness 'grasped' them at the point in time when their relationship with the human family had become stuck.

Regarding this matter of perception, I should add that after three years of regular visits to South America, I have learned to perceive the elemental beings outside of any cultural pattern, by just focussing upon the practical role they play in the landscape as an aspect of the earth consciousness. Only by seeing elemental beings in this way can we transcend the basic difference between the modes of perception according to European or American patterns.

Our current challenge as human beings is that our process of individuation has in the meanwhile evolved to the point where we ought not to lean any more on mass patterns, but instead create our own personal language to perceive the reality around us. Right now, we are just beginning to learn how to become the conscious co-creators of our own perceptions. As a result, we have to be prepared to deal with a world which in the near future will lose the uniformity we know today, and realize a variability beyond our imagination.

In practice, this means that when we do exercises to help us perceive the invisible dimensions of reality, we should not direct them towards seeing the world exactly as others do, but rather to finding out which language of perception suits us best. We can detect the best choice for ourselves by observing our reactions to the different phenomena we attune to. Once you get the sense of 'your path', you should stick to it, explore it in detail, discover exercises to develop it, and trust that it can convey to you that face of reality which is important to you.

For example, during my seminars on perception I have encountered individuals who can perceive invisible phenomena perfectly by the different reactions of their physical body. They can observe the movements of their hands, legs, hips, etc. The whole skeleton is like a sensitive pendulum system. If we allow it to move freely within the vibrational pattern of the place where we are standing, we can read much from its movements.

Others prefer to observe their emotional sensations and so perceive through the language of the qualities involved. Their perceptions refer rather to the psyche of a place than to its power structure. Still others concentrate on inner visions. In their case, their consciousness translates the incoming informational stream into colors, light forms or images. And it is also possible to combine all these different methods and so attain perceptions that are diversified in different layers, and therefore quite accurate. This is the method I have adopted.

Now, if perception is becoming so extremely individualized, what are the criteria to determine what is true and what is hallucination or ego-trip?

First of all, it is advisable to work in small groups and talk about your perceptions, compare them, and work to find the common denominator that relates to the objective essence of the phenomena perceived. Be honest with yourself and others. If as a culture we were to decide to abolish the absolute predominance of 'objective reality' by also integrating with it the subjective quality of individual perception, then moral attitude will gain immense importance. It will be seen to be the main assurance for the credibility of a person's insights. This in turn emphasizes the need to work constantly on our personal and inner development in order not to get stuck in illusions and philosophical concepts that may distort our perceptions and affect what we put forward as our view of reality.

Furthermore, while working to refine our perceptions, it is advisable to keep your particular aspect of awareness in reserve, as it were. You let it 'stand by' to watch over the perception process, but you do not give it the right to interfere. In this way you can keep a proper distance and yet become aware of potential dangers to the credibility of your perceptions. It is not always possible to be well grounded and connected on all levels and, as a result, our perceptions may be overwhelmed by fantasies.

Keep a watch also over the degree to which the information you gain is already known to your consciousness. Be aware that the earth cosmos is so perfect that there are no two places or two moments which are alike. Each one is unique and each bears the stamp of a different quality even if it is related to others of its kind. You should become alarmed if you notice that a pattern is repeating itself so often as to become boring. The truthfulness of an insight can be recognized by the breath of innocence and surprise conveyed by each perception. The intimate feeling of surprise denotes that we are indeed being confronted with a true moment or phenomenon of life. These are always new and can never be known to us before we have experienced them. Those things which can be known in advance are mind-created patterns and preconceptions, and not the truth of a living experience.

Exercises in Grounding and Connecting

Before they begin the process of perceiving the invisible layers of reality, I advise people to do some personal grounding and connecting exercises. As inhabitants of the modern world, we are used to living within the mental framework of our mind and do not notice that we are walking, thinking and feeling within an artificial world structure, separated from the earth cosmos. According to the criteria of energy, emotion and spirit, we are moving in the void rather than walking on the ground. So how can we adequately perceive the subtle dimensions of nature, the landscape or a fellow human being when we are not inwardly connected to those dimensions?

Grounding exercise 1

Imagine that you are a beautiful tree with roots going deep down into the earth to connect you with the planet's powers and emotional qualities, and with branches reaching high towards the heavens to connect you to the stars and their powers and spiritual qualities.

Hold this sense of identity in your imagination for a space, while you stand consciously on the ground (don't stiffen your knees!) and invest yourself in deep heartfelt feelings of devotion for your Mother Earth and Father Sky. By doing this you will make the connection, not just on the power level, but also on the emotional and spiritual ones.

Grounding exercise 2

While you are breathing in, imagine that you are drawing your breath from the depths of the earth, and while breathing out, imagine that you are releasing your breath towards the heights of the cosmos.

Pause for a moment and then do the opposite: draw your breath from the cosmos, and while breathing out let it glide into the earth. Pause for a moment and then start from the beginning again. Go on breathing like this for a while.

Grounding exercise 3

While standing up and giving your attention and respect to the ground beneath you, imagine that the soil under your feet is broken up into little pieces like crumbs of bread.

Let these crumbs of earth rise slowly up through your body till they reach above and beyond the top of your head. Pause for a moment like this, and then let them glide down into the ground again. Pause again for a moment and do it twice more.

You can do these kinds of exercises anywhere without upsetting the people around you — who, after all, don't know what's going on. The first two exercises should work even if the floor you are standing on is high above the ground. Just take good care that your consciousness goes down deep enough to reach the soil beneath. But if you find yourself in a good working space, it would be as well to add some of the hologramic exercises described Chapter 5.

I also advise you to round off these connecting exercises by reaffirming the wholeness of your personal holon. This exercise is known as the Cloak of Protection Exercise. It is based on the idea that the whole of our personal body, with its energetic, emotional and other dimensions, is rounded off and surrounded by an egg-shaped cloak of protection. This represents the skin of our subtle bodies. Just as the skin protects our physical body from all kinds of infection, the cloak of light protects our fields of power and emotion from invasion by foreign energies and information. For this purpose it is composed of many layers of light filters that screen out potentially damaging vibrations. Imagine what an important task 'the skin' of our personal holon has to play in an era overloaded with all kinds of radio waves, telecommunication channels, distorted power fields, horrific emotional clouds, etc!

On the other hand, just as the skin makes it possible for the body to breathe, the cloak of protection permits the passage of 'good' vibrations and so facilitates our complete communication with the world around us. This is the second reason why it is necessary to ensure that one's cloak of protection is not weakened or damaged. Look to the safety of your most personal home!

Cloak of protection exercise

Take a moment to center yourself in your heart. Then imagine that you are standing within an egg-shaped cloak of protection which is structured in the form of a light membrane. It extends around the body at a distance a bit beyond the reach of your hand and also to about 2 1/2 feet (80 cm) below your feet. Make sure that the cloak is beautifully rounded off – including the area of your back.

But remember that a person, though protected, is not entirely closed off in their wholeness. A light axis running parallel to your spine simultaneously connects you to the center of the earth and the heart of the universe.

When we have absorbed the theory of multidimensional perception and completed the preparatory exercises, we are ready to begin the exercises on perception. I have divided them into seven chapters to indicate the different methods of approaching the joy of perceiving.

Chapter one: using your body as an instrument

1. Find somewhere out in the open, close your eyes for a moment and attune to the essence of the place. Then open your eyes and without turning round, direct your attention all around you. Do this again and again, scanning sounds, feelings, visual imprints, etc. Listen to the wholeness of the ambience around you and try to complement the physical perceptions by intuiting the invisible dimensions at your sides or behind your back. You can do the same exercise while walking through the countryside. But then you have to walk very slowly and consciously.

2. Use your hands to go into the atmosphere of the place that you wish to explore, and touch its invisible structures and qualities to try to figure out how it feels. Learn to distinguish the differences that occur from place to place.

3. Stand in the place which you are exploring and relax your body; attune to your surroundings, and set your body free to move in the rhythms of the place. Learn the language of your body movements. For this purpose one may use the movements of one hand only, of both hands, or of the whole body.

Chapter two: observing the emotional qualities

1. Center yourself in your heart, and then open to the place you are exploring without any expectations or preconceptions. While you are opening yourself, you should stay in your heart and listen to your surroundings. Do not start to explore on your own, but let the place talk to you. Wait patiently for the place to reveal itself to you in its own way.

2. In an effort to consciously avoid putting your own projections on your observations, turn your back on the place you are interested in. Try to get clear about the characteristic quality of the place by 'observing' it through your back.

3. Approach a shrub or a tree with hanging branches and take the very end branch with its top leaves lightly between your hands. Be loving and sensitive to your plant-sister. Listen the feelings that may stream back to you through your hands. This exercise can well serve to contact the tree spirit.

Chapter three: freeing consciousness to move about

1. Now you introduce your different chakras into the perception process, treating them as if they were organs of perception. The heart center and solar plexus[2] are especially appropriate for this process. Place your awareness in a selected chakra and stay focused there for a while. Then withdraw your consciousness to the space behind the chakra so as to distance yourself a little from its center, and from that point 'look' towards the phenomenon you wish to explore.

2. Choose a flower and observe it for a while. Then imagine that your consciousness is like a bee, so that you enter the flower's space like a bee in search of honey. While you are inside, you should feel around you to get the experience of the flower's inner space.

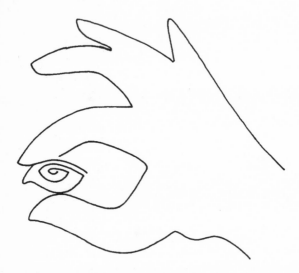

3. Imagine there is an eye located within your heart. Imagine that you take that eye between your thumb and forefinger and 'drive' with it through your surroundings, 'looking' at the place from different angles.

---

2 This exercise is described in detail in my book *Healing the Heart of the Earth*, page 150.

Chapter four: turning space around — experiencing the other (invisible) side of an environment

Refer to (a), (b) and (c) in the drawing.

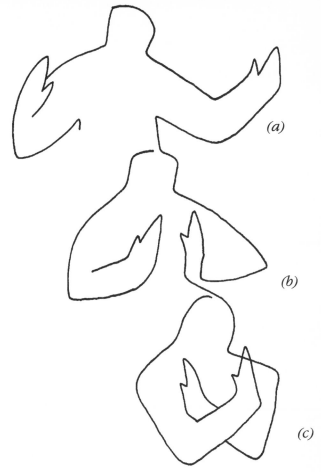

1. Stretch out your hands to either side and imagine that you are touching both sides of the place you want to observe (a). Identify with the place just as you see it. Then draw your hands together till they start to overlap each other (b). While you are drawing them together, imagine that you are condensing the visible aspect of the place down to point zero. Then close your eyes and look/feel through the 'window' created by your overlapping hands (c).

2. Imagine that you are inhaling the surrounding ambience as it exists in its physical form. Turn it around within your heart so that the inside becomes the outside. Then close your eyes, exhale it inside-out and observe how the reality feels.

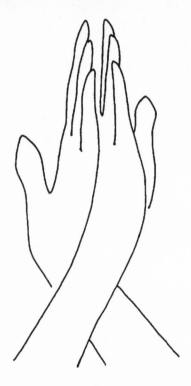

3. Place your hands palm to palm. Then turn them around so that they touch each other back to back. In the same moment, through resonance, the polarity of the place also tends to switch, so that by closing your eyes you can get an insight into the essence of the 'other side' of the place.

Chapter five: exercises in identification

These kinds of exercises help the observer become one with the observed, and also to find a way to demonstrate this oneness. Because of our manifested oneness with the observed, we will naturally receive insights into its essence.

1. Think of the way indigenous people decorate themselves

with birds' feathers, shells, pieces of tree bark, etc., and how they put bright colors upon their faces... Do the same in your own way, though not physically but in your imagination. The purpose of this is to show the elemental world that aspect of yourself which is naturally part of the nature kingdom.

In response, the world of nature will also be eager to show you that aspect of itself which we don't usually perceive. Make sure that you act swiftly when decorating yourself, then close your eyes and listen without doubts or hesitation.

2. Rest for a while and observe the features in the place or landscape around you. Then close your eyes and integrate those features into your body as if they were a part of your constitution. Do it swiftly so as not to lose the momentum of their reality. Afterwards you should feel and 'look' around you to get to know the place in its essence. It will be revealed to you if you have previously identified yourself properly as a particle of its wholeness.

3. Stand in front of a tree and imagine that your legs are covered with the same kind of bark as the tree. Imagine your body taking on the characteristic shape of that particular tree. Then open yourself to the tree spirit to receive its message.

Repeat the exercise in front of different kinds of trees to sensitize yourself to the diversity of their vibrations.

Chapter six: call on your spiritual guides for help

As we will discuss in depth later, each one of us is surrounded by invisible helpers. If we are ready to ask, they will be eager to help us through our process of getting to know the invisible dimensions of a place.

But be aware that the process of deepening your perception is one path that you have to walk by yourself. Nobody else can walk it for you. It follows that your spiritual guides may be unable to help you if you try to rely too much on their abilities, or if you use them to avoid the effort of learning for yourself. If you were to force yourself on them, the perceptions you received might be severely distorted or even false. Be conscious of this possibility!

1. Approach the place that you wish to explore, close your eyes, attune to it, and ask your personal invisible helpers to guide you to the point where you can best experience the particular aspect of the place that you are seeking to know more fully.

When you feel the impulse to move forward — either in your hand or in your emotions — open your eyes, and go and follow the impulse to the place where it disappears. Stay there and explore the place by means of one of the exercises proposed above.

2. To talk with the place and get specific information about it, one needs to contact the elemental beings who are responsible for it, or its spiritual guardians. In order to enter into communication, you should attune to the place first and then inwardly address the source you would like to talk to, explain your purpose, and give thanks.

Next, raise your consciousness up to the high angelic level of existence. Visualize bright white light in order to secure the highest possible level of contact, so that you don't end up with your communication stuck in some lower emotional tangle. Then go down again, carrying the quality you have achieved in the angelic realm into your heart. Rest there and start your discourse. Be attentive to the sensations, feelings and images that may pop up within your psyche.

Chapter seven: intuitive approach

There is little that needs comment in this seventh chapter. Realize that there is a facet of ourselves which allows us to know anything, before we have even had the courage to ask about it. Be aware of that level in yourself and watch for the unexpected notions, ideas, images, signs... that may appear. Do not neglect them as something coincidental, but rather consider them to be expressions of your higher self. You will recognize them by the special flavor of infinity which they carry. Learn to listen to your intuition, and make this learning a permanent exercise in which you also involve your dreams and events from everyday life.

Chapter Four

Earth Changes —
Continuing the Story

In February 1998 I realized that the earth changes had begun their 'labor pains'. Since then I have been desperately seeking some key or 'timetable' which would help me understand what is going on at any given moment, and what the course of future events might be. I was simply unable to believe that humanity would be subjected to such a turmoil as may be provoked by the expected undoing of the earth holon without being provided with some sort of compass to help us know at each step where we are.

In fact, for the past few years I have been nursing an intuition that the Western culture's most reliable key is hidden within the ancient text of the Revelation of St. John. This is an exalted, in places also bizarre, composition of visions, insights and channeled speech which St. John, a pupil of Jesus the Christ, received at the age of 90 while staying on the Greek island of Patmos. If one listens inwardly to the text, which is usually called 'The Apocalypse', one gets the convincing impression that it is one of those divine messages which are given to humanity in advance to prepare us for the future ages.

Looking at the composition of the Bible[1] as a whole, one can see a surprising relationship between the first Book of Moses — which we call 'Genesis' — placed at the beginning of the biblical corpus, and the Apocalypse at its end. A sacred tree plays the central role in both these texts. In the case of Genesis, it is the Tree of Knowledge which is placed in the middle of the Paradise, and

---

1 The term 'Bible' here refers to the Christian canon, which includes the texts of the New Testament.

in the case of the Apocalypse, it is the Tree of Life which stands in the center of the New Jerusalem, itself a symbol of the future earth cosmos.

The Tree of the Knowledge of Good and Evil — that is its full name — stands for that phase of human evolution in which we are confronted with the challenge of our own freedom, the freedom to choose between good and evil and decide how to act according to their criteria, without being guided 'from outside' towards the 'right' decision. Through the initiatory act of 'eating' the fruit from the Tree of Knowledge, our ancestors, symbolically represented by Adam and Eve, demonstrated that human beings had grown sufficiently to enter into a new phase of evolution, one where we needed to learn to stand on our own feet, create from our own vision, and love from the inspiration of our own heart.

According to the Bible story, the initiatory act of entering this new phase of human evolution was followed by what is called the 'Expulsion from Paradise'. Translated from the language of symbols, the 'Expulsion from Paradise' might mean that there was a decisive change in the earthly environment within which human evolution had developed up till that moment. Beforehand, it was characterized by the quality of a paradise, where human beings were as if spoiled, permanently bathed in the sun of the Divine Presence and the love of Mother Earth. Afterwards, the earth displays the harsh and challenging face of our material environment.

As a symbol, 'Paradise' stands for a world structure in which the emotional, spiritual and energetic levels were so balanced as to form a kind of womb where the early phases of human evolution could take place. Like a child floating in the waters of the mother's womb, human beings were cradled by the pliant, peaceful quality of the earth's emotional level, which was the ruling aspect of that era.

This changed drastically when we started to incarnate on the physical level. This new step in our evolution must have been accompanied by a spectacular change in the environment within which our evolution was taking place, a change which is concealed behind the label 'Expulsion from Paradise'. Since then, myths worldwide tell of 'Paradise Lost'.

From the scientific point of view, of course, it appears uncon-scionable to link the relatively short history of the human race with the immense time-span of earth's geological evolution. Yet there is no contradiction if we agree on the concept that life has a multi-dimensional character. It is perfectly possible for the earth to have been developing its physical body for billions of years while human evolution was proceeding simultaneously on anoth-er — in this case emotional — level of existence. Only after nature, through the evolution of the primates, had prepared the kind of physical body which corresponded to the needs of the new step in human evolution, did human beings start to 'come down' and incarnate on the material level of the planet.

From that moment forward our prehistory started, as we know from archaeological research. We find small groups of peo-ple inhabiting distant places of the planet and carving their first tools from bones, wood and stone... Yet, after millennia of evolu-tion, these same people became — through the power of the rational mind — perfect masters of the physical world. Finally, in the 20th century we have developed our technologies to the point that we can play with matter at will and even destroy the planet's life in a split second. It is obvious that we have outgrown the 'classroom' that was created for us when we were 'expelled from Paradise'.

One can well imagine a scenario whereby, to bestow a new classroom upon humanity and prevent a universal catastrophe, the earth and her spiritual guides have triggered — now at the threshold of the 3rd millennium — a far-reaching cycle of earth changes. It will bring to an end the segregated physical ambience where we have lived since we left the womb of Paradise. It is this same cycle of change that is directing us towards the gate of the multi-dimensional future earth. In biblical language, it is called the 'New Jerusalem'. It is this New Jerusalem which is said to be built around the second of the Bible's two sacred trees, the Tree of Life.

If the first words in the Bible preserve the memory of the complicated process of human evolution as it settled down on the physical plane of existence — a process that has been proceeding through past millennia and is in part still continuing — the

Revelation of St John, positioned at the end of the Bible, gives us insights into another chapter of our evolutionary adventure. This is leading humanity towards a 'new Heaven and a new Earth' (Rev 21:1), and is a chapter that is about to start now, in our present time.

With this understanding of the Bible's composition from Genesis to the Apocalypse, I was not too much surprised when Julius, my counselor from the nature kingdom, pointed to the apocalyptic story of the Seven Seals as the key to understanding the different phases of the earth changes that I had been experiencing over the past two years. It was no more than a hint that I got from my friend. Yet I felt that within the impulse had been encoded a whole new way of looking at the text of the Apocalypse.

I kept the impulse treasured like a jewel in my consciousness while I ran home to get my Bible. I brought it to the top of the hill where I had had my conversation with Julius. Then I started to re-read the Sixth Chapter of Revelation entitled 'The Lamb breaks the Seals'[2], but this time I viewed its message in the mirror of my experiences of the earth changes.

The story starts in the Fifth Chapter where a book is being held in the divine hand. It tells of future events and is sealed with seven seals. Let us listen to the words of St. John: "And I saw a mighty angel who called out in a loud voice, 'Who is fit to open the book and break its seals?' And no one in Heaven or upon earth or under the earth was able to open the book, or even to look at it. I began to weep bitterly because no one could be found fit to open the book, or even to look at it..." (Rev 5:2)

Then, unlooked for, there appears a lamb standing in the very center of the divine throne. It is not just an ordinary lamb such as we know standing in our hills and meadows. It has inherited the memory of having at one time been slaughtered. Also it is endowed with seven horns and seven eyes, which stand for the seven divine qualities. Both symbols lead me to believe that the lamb represents the universal power which guides human evolution and which the Western tradition calls 'The Christ'. It is the

2 The texts quoted are taken from *The New Testament in Modern English*, translated by J.B. Phillips, first published by Collins & Son, London, 1960.

Christ power which embodies the divine qualities of creation in order to implement them within the universe as a whole. It is also the power of the Christ that incarnated in Palestine through the individuality of a man called Jesus who came to teach people, and ultimately be slaughtered on the cross.

But, we may ask, if we have to deal with a divine power, why is it here presented in animal form? It is because, in opening the book of future events related to the earth changes, we have to do with the elemental (i.e., earthly) aspect of the Christ power. One could say that only by entering the material level of existence by taking on a human body could the divine impulse 'move' the earth's evolution onward to a new cycle of change. Only after the divine power had become 'a lamb' was it possible for the Christ to open the seven seals which conceal the future transfigurations of the earth cosmos.

When the lamb broke the first of the seven seals, John saw "a white horse. Its rider carried a bow, and he was given a crown. He rode out conquering and bent on conquest." (Rev 6:2)

The joyous image of the rider on the white horse denotes the first phase of the earth changes, which I perceived between February 10th and April 20th, 1998. This was when the ground radiation was gradually changing till ultimately the earth was 'crowned' with a new aura. Its main quality relates to the element of air, symbolized in this case by the bow, i.e., a device to shoot through the air.

When the lamb broke the second seal, "another horse came forth, red in color. Its rider was given power to deprive the earth of peace, so that man should kill each other. A huge sword was put into his hand." (Rev 6:4)

According to the inspiration conveyed by Julius, the rider on the red horse symbolizes the second phase of the process of earth changes. This is the phase marked by the appearance of the 'new powers'. I described them at length in the first chapter, showing how these reveal the quality of the primeval powers of creation. They only know the holistic universe and are incognizant of the divisions and structures characteristic of the way that human civilization deals with the earth cosmos. For this reason, the new powers are a threat to the alienated human world. Their appearance on the earth's surface seems enough to "deprive the earth of peace."

Up to this point, the suggestions made by my invisible friend had been quite acceptable, indicating how the first two of the seven seals might be used as a mirror to understand the recent earth changes. But I was most interested in information about the third seal, for this should tell me what was happening right then in the third phase of the earth's transfiguration. I consider this phase to have started with the solar eclipse of August 11th, 1999. It was a month later that I was conferring with Julius about the seven seals. At the time I had some perceptions of the new phenomena which did not fit with the first two seals, but I was far from understanding the essence of the new phase.

I had a strong feeling that, to understand this new phase, the 'old sage' from the elemental world was urging me to trust the succession of the seven seals. It followed that I should continue to ponder those verses of Revelation which refer to the third seal, even though, whenever I had read them earlier, my mind had thought them quite ridiculous: "I looked again and there before my eyes was a black horse. Its rider had a pair of scales in his hand, and I heard a voice...saying: 'A quart of wheat for a shilling, and three quarts of barley for a shilling — but no tampering with the oil or the wine!" (Rev 6:6) While I was giving my attention to the text, Julius brought the symbol of the scales to my consciousness, giving it special emphasis. I also felt that he was suggesting that I understand the scales in the sense of the balancing and shifting of etheric masses.

I would have been quite unable to understand his meaning if I had not noticed gigantic shifts occurring within the organism of earth's ambience immediately after the celebrated solar eclipse of August 11th. For ages past people had thought this solar eclipse might be destined to be fatal for the earth, because on that precise day the main planets would form a perfect cross in the sky. At the same time, the threatening shadow of the moon would move diagonally across Europe, loosing the earth for a moment from the dense ties that connect our planet to the powers of the sun.

The changes that I observed later must have happened in the time-span covered by the eclipse, when the earth got those precious moments of freedom from its solar bonds. According to my observations, the planet used them well, reorganizing itself. Solar eclipses come and go, but this time one coincided uniquely with the onset of a new cycle of earth changes. It even seems that the planet might have consciously used the opportunity offered by the solar eclipse, coupled with the unique planetary configuration, to initiate a new cycle of transformation.

As an example of my observations, I should like to recount the reorganization and rebalancing of the etheric ambience of my country, Slovenia. I know it best because at the time of the eclipse I was observing the process from my home. Before the transformation of the etheric base of its physical ambience, the light-body of Slovenia was organized in separate units that were related to the main sources of the powers of the Four Elements in the country. The geological basin where the capital Ljubljana is located is somewhat central to this configuration and held a balancing role.

When I tuned into the etheric ambience of Slovenia after the solar eclipse, I perceived a different configuration of its etheric masses. A light cupola had been formed over the Ljubljana basin mentioned above. During the days following, this 'cupola' proceeded to stretch deep underground, eventually to be rounded off to form a perfect sphere with a diameter of about 40 kilometers. This sphere now represents one pole of the country's power balance, while the other is formed by the powers of the Four Elements arranged around it in the form of mighty belts of energy. Their etheric structure has been gradually reinforced to form a kind of amplified ring around the central sphere. I could feel a fresh and extremely vivid energy exchange between the two polarized features. *(See illustration on page 76.)*

Even more exciting was the occurrence that covered the whole central part of Europe. Prior to the solar eclipse on August 11th, regions like Bavaria, Switzerland, Austria, Bohemia and Slovenia had been closed up within their own power structures. As a result, the ambience of Central Europe was extremely fragmented. Only by viewing it from high above could I feel its unified spiritual essence encoded in a kind of light capsule. But there was

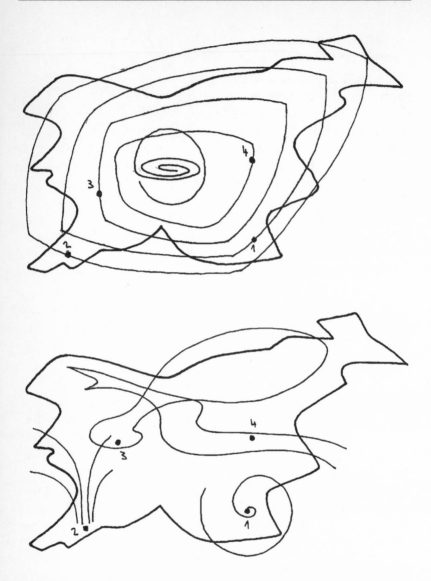

*The etheric configuration of my country Slovenia before
(below) and after (above) the solar eclipse of August 11th 1999.
The borders of the country are marked with a thicker line. The
numbers denote the dominant quality of one of the Four
Elements in a certain region: 1 stands for Element Earth, 2 for
Element Fire, 3 for Element Air and 4 for Element Water.*

no connection between this lofty coded information and the actual ambience that ought to have embodied it.

Soon after the shadow of the eclipse had passed over Central Europe from the northwest and glided on to the southeast, I noticed that strong belts of the fire element had encompassed the central area of the continent. A strong power activity now made itself felt within the central area of Europe. In the days following, the light capsule positioned high above the area started to descend. As it settled downward, it became clothed in a broad pillar of white light which eventually touched the earth over a circular area extending from Bern, Switzerland, in the west, to Prague, Bohemia, in the east, and from Zagreb, Croatia, in the south, to Frankfurt, Germany, in the north.

After 'touching' the ground, the light pillar continued its descent into the depth of the earth, flaring outwards like the bell of a trumpet. This was obviously designed to anchor the newly gained unity of Europe's previously fragmented core deep in the 'underground' of the continent'.

At this point you may be asking yourself, what in heaven's name am I talking about? Let me summarize the information presented so far. In Chapter Two I explained in some detail the nature of the planet's geomantic constitution, relating it to the powers of the earth and its intelligence. First, I introduced the concept of the earth's nourishing system, through which the planet provides the indivisible basic power which nourishes all the levels and forms of its life. Second, I talked in detail about the earth's vital-energy organs which distribute life-power over its surface to keep it and its beings alive. The functioning of these organs can be compared to the chakras of the human body.

Next we broached the idea of the planetary consciousness which imbues each aspect of the earth cosmos with intelligence. Individualized in relatively separate units, which we used to call nature spirits or elemental beings, this consciousness impregnates each manifestation of life on the planet, even the tiniest, with intelligence.

Up to this point we have been exploring the earth cosmos and have come to know the powers of the planet and its consciousness. Next we will get to understand its light-body. This is not a new concept, since much was said in Chapter One about the four elements and the radiation streams coming from the ground, and both phenomena are connected with the light-body of the earth.

The ground radiation represents one aspect of the planet's aura. The aura is a power field composed of many layers which permeates the earth's geological body and its atmosphere. The ground radiation is a manifestation of the densest layer of the earth's aura and extends only a little way beyond the physical body of the earth. However, there are finer layers which extend high into the atmosphere, or even into its cosmic ambience.

The etheric configurations which I was describing in relation to Slovenia and Central Europe represent another, more basic aspect of the light-body of the earth. I discovered this aspect a few years ago while preparing for some earth healing projects. To feel out a place's general state of health, I am in the habit of attuning to its totality by scanning the geological maps of the country involved. While my hands work over a map, I can feel certain features, one could say invisible forms, that constitute a framework within which all the geomantic phenomena are located. I have started to call this the 'etheric basis of an ambience'. Over the course of time I have also noticed that the light features of the etheric basis always relate to one of the four elements.

To give an example, I would invite you for a moment to come with me to Hanover, Germany. This is an ancient merchant city, renowned for the World Exhibition hosted there in the year 2000. The etheric basis of the city's ambience takes the form of a cross, in the middle of which is located a double cupola so large that the whole city center fits within it.

One branch of the cross is formed by a stream of liquid ether which follows the course of the river Leine as it meanders through the structure of the town in a general north-south direction (Water Element). The other branch is made up of a stream of air ether which is introduced into the city's ambience by the Benther hill in the west and the Eilenriede forest in the east (Air Element).

The town church is located in the center of this cross formation. It has a mighty bell tower which embodies a vertical axis

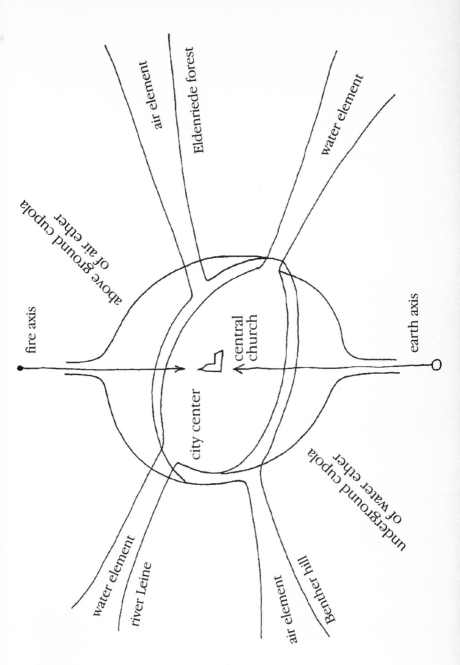

The light body of Hanover, Germany,
an ancient merchant city positioned on the river Leine.

composed of fiery ethers descending from the breadths of the universe, and of earth ethers ascending from the depths of the earth (Elements of Fire and Earth). This axis, through which heaven and earth communicate, seems to be the reason why the Air Element forms a light cupola around that exact spot. It extends above the ground, and the medieval culture used it as a safe space within which the old Hanover could develop successfully. The Water Element forms a complementary cupola which is positioned beneath the city. It is clear that the city has occupied a perfectly balanced ambience where the four elements meet and interact. Yet, because no care has been taken of the etheric basis within which Hanover's structures stand, this balance has to a great degree been lost.

To show how the etheric basis of an ambience may differ from place to place, let me introduce the main features of my view of Manhattan, New York, referring specifically to the levels under discussion. The geological form of Manhattan Island can be compared to the shape of the human body, with its feet in the north and its head on the southern side. Interestingly, as relates to its inhale/exhale circuit, the tips of the 'feet' connect the island with the depths of the earth, while its 'head', in the area of Battery Park, displays an upwardly moving surge which connects with the breadths of the universe. Since both streams also interact, there is a circular movement of the Air Element's powers around the island. The Indians called Manhattan, 'Turtle Island'.

Since Manhattan Island is a gigantic monolith of granite, etherically rooted deep down in the fiery layer of earth's core, the Fire Element has a very powerful presence there. These fiery powers surge out of every etheric pore in the granite body of the island to form kinds of rounded etheric sheets that permeate Manhattan's atmosphere. They have been very much broken and distorted by the pressure of the structure and dynamic of the massive city, yet they still represent the creative power for which New York City is renowned worldwide.

Since Manhattan island lies between three rivers, the East River, Harlem River and Hudson River, there is a strong polarization between the Elements of Fire and Water, and this further reinforces its powers. Seen with the inner sight, the Water

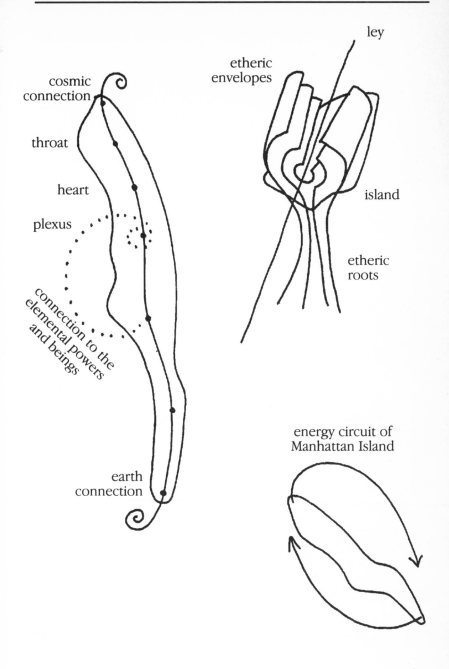

cosmic connection

throat

heart

plexus

connection to the elemental powers and beings

earth connection

ley

etheric envelopes

island

etheric roots

energy circuit of Manhattan Island

Insights into the light body of Manhattan Island , New York.

Element forms a polarized framework which embraces the island and holds the overbearing powers of Fire in balance.

During the past age of our evolution we have concentrated more and more of our attention on the physical plane, finally to the exclusion of all else. As a result we have totally forgotten that, besides its pattern of geological features, the life of a landscape has another kind of framework. This is the light-body composed of etheric masses and fields which offer the opportunity for the life processes to manifest, connect with each other and be properly balanced. The physical body composed of mountains, rivers, etc., is of course important for the grounding of life on the material level, but without its etheric counterpart it would be deprived of life itself.

My friend from the nature kingdom had given me the inspiration about the sign of the third apocalyptic seal, and this suggested that shifts should occur in the etheric masses, or light-body, of the earth. I could feel them happening around Christmas, 1999. They started with peculiar changes in the general quality of the Earth Element. It became weak and soft, which is very unusual for the element which we mainly experience through the solid forms of the material world. By December 11th the element of earth had already become so extremely weak that I could feel hardly its presence at all.

On that day I had gone with my wife Marika to the foot of a mighty mountain in Carinthia, dedicated in ancient times to the Goddess. Its name is Peca and its present day destiny is to stand right between Austria and Slovenia, so the national border divides it. Since summer 1999, we had been carrying out an 'acupuncture of the earth' project there on both sides of the border, and we were now visiting the place to continue our work. The aim is to transcend the artificial obstacle that the border represents in a landscape that should be considered as a whole[3].

That day I looked with my inner eye towards the broad peak of the sacred mountain, which is similar to a volcanic crater, and I was shocked. Peca was sending me a perfectly clear picture.

3 The Lithopuncture Project, carried out in Carinthia on both sides of the border between Austria and Slovenia, was organized by the Galery Falke, Bleiburg/Loibach, Austria.

I saw a young boy being born out of the 'crater'. While the upper part of the body had already been successfully delivered, the birth process was severely stuck at the level of the boy's hips. I saw the boy twisting and curving and bending, yet the mountain could not carry through with 'her' birthing process. The image was accompanied by a feeling of extreme urgency.

We returned to my home at Sempas in Slovenia the next day, and I felt that the power of the Earth Element had nearly disappeared there too. On the other hand, the presence of the Fire Element was far too strong. I could both feel and see flames of etheric fire flickering with great abandon everywhere in the atmosphere. The situation was one of extreme unbalance. I could feel it even in my own backbone which started to bend in a very strange way, especially if I tried to attune myself to the earth axis. In the following weeks I had the sensation of being put on the rack and tortured.

I took all this as a sign that the cooperation of people of goodwill might be urgently needed, and on December 13th, 1999, my daughter Ana asked the angelic world for an explanation. The answer told us that a turbulent time lies ahead. The earth is moving through another cycle of changes. The problem is that humanity persists in staying out of the process, as though unready to take part in the next step. In consequence, the human race runs the danger of losing its connection with the earth's evolution altogether. Our process of change should run parallel, or at the least follow the earth's transformations, adjusting constantly to its mutations. But this option is exactly what humanity is ignoring at this time.

The angelic message underlines the fact that while the human evolution is of course autonomous to a large degree, yet it is still part of a larger whole. If we lose our inner connections with the earth, it will not be possible for humanity to participate any longer in the planet's web of life. We have been warned that in the days ahead there exists a real danger of such an ultimate split.

We need to work consciously to make a personal reconnection with the earth. This effort requires the participation of an increasing number of people. One should make the space available to the powers of the earth to become part of one's own energy field, and repeat this exercise over and over again. People should regularly work on sensing the presence of the earth's power-field and emotional field within their own beings, and on anchoring them deep within their body. Then, we should reconnect vertically downwards to the heart core of the earth and upwards to the heavens, and visualize all people as connected through this kind of light axis to the center to the earth. Finally, we should imagine that the core of the earth is shining like a sun, with the result that the axis of each human being becomes a ray of that sun.

Now that I had become that much clearer about the present third phase of the earth changes (which has just unfolded its potential during the year-end transition from 1999 to 2000), I was eager to know what the next phase would be. But at this point Julius made it clear that I was on the wrong path. Without my noticing my error, I was trying to infiltrate linear patterns into a process which is evolving on a cyclical basis and is simultaneously involving different layers. My head wants to see more and more interesting changes, one following after another, while my body is stuck in a physical reality which as yet has not changed at all.

My friend from the nature kingdom followed his criticism with a bunch of suggestions, as to how I might better understand the present situation. First of, all we should be aware that the changes are evolving on other levels than the one which appears, at any given moment, to be the active one. Different strands of the process are in progress all the time, even if they sometimes seem to disappear from the surface of events.

While it is true that the events of the first three apocalyptic seals have entered the process in separate successive phases, as presented here, we should be aware that on the other hand they are all proceeding simultaneously, complementing and supporting each other. It is illusory to believe that we have resolved some of them successfully when there are others still waiting to pour down on our heads.

Julius also tried to calm my overcharged emotions, cooling my impatience. I felt like crying out at the prospect that humanity might miss the most exciting era of the earth changes, and simply not notice the subtle processes which I am describing.

"What we are witnessing at present are really the preparations for the main changes yet to come. Elemental beings are being trained to become 'midwifes' of the earth's rebirth. The necessary powers are even now concentrating on the planet's surface. People are alarmed and their consciousness is being prepared, so that humanity will be ready to accept the changes and collaborate with them as they progress. When the main changes start, they will be obvious on the physical level too."

When I realized that I should change my question from, "What comes next?" to "Which processes of the earth changes can we recognize, in addition to the three already known?", the path was opened to a discussion of the fourth of the apocalyptic seals. Let me first quote the corresponding words from Revelation: "Then, when he broke the fourth seal...there appeared a horse sickly green in color. The name of its rider was death, and the grave followed close behind him. A quarter of the earth was put into their power, to kill with the sword, by famine, by violence, and through the wild beasts of the earth." (Rev 6:7)

It is always difficult for a human being to face the phenomenon of death. During the next phase, is our race going to succumb to a massive wave of deaths? I felt that Julius was trying to stem my rising tide of fear by reminding me that we are here dealing with a symbolic language and not with banal predictions of the future.

He suggested rather that the text points towards the overthrow of the world's structure as we know it today. We used to know a dimension which we called the 'world of the dead'. In the current epoch this has been pushed outside the boundaries of existence and encapsulated in a separate closed 'underworld'. This will open up, to be integrated into the normal life cycle. And what we know as material reality, the one that is perceptible to our physical senses, will take an opposite path and turn inward. This will enable it to reach a new and more concentrated level of development. The consciousness of the earth on the other hand will 'overflow' and fill up all the interstices between the different dimensions to facilitate communication between them. This will enable people to be conscious of all the different levels of existence simultaneously.

The image of the 'grave following close behind' refers to the opening of the gates between those dimensions which have been closed during the past epoch when the rational mind governed our perception of reality. When it says that death would get to rule over 'a quarter of the earth', this symbolizes the return of the 'underworld' to human awareness, taking back that portion of reality which naturally belongs to it.

On December 29th, 1998, a dream made me conscious for the first time of this rather obscure phase of the earth changes. I experienced myself as being part of a group of people sentenced to death. Not only was I upset, I was also angry because I could not understand why I should have to die. Then I was shown the gigantic stump of a lime tree which had been cut down ages before, and was now overgrown with a thick layer of moss. Even though I knew the place well, I had never noticed that the stump was there.

I was deeply moved by my close meeting with death, yet I knew I should not worry. The dream's purpose in making me 'smell' death's presence was quite clear. It was directing my attention to the world of the deceased, which in the ancient cultures was recognized as part of the united human family. In my dream that world was symbolized by the huge lime tree. But in the meanwhile the tree, representing the integral human community, has been cut down and our ancestors pushed out of the role they had once occupied in relation to the society of the living.

In effect, all members of the human family who once lived on the earth — if they are not presently in incarnation — partake of the world of ancestors. Imagine what a wealth of knowledge, experience and wisdom is stored there! It could provide much precious help to the incarnated portion of humanity as we struggle with the problems of cultural growth and individual development. As much as we on this side of the veil are limited in our perceptions and insights because of the bonds of space and time, the ancestors who abide in the all-embracing ambience of the spiritual world are free to know almost anything, for they take part in the wisdom of eternity.

Both halves of the human family, the deceased and the living, once used to complement each other. Each of the ancient cultures developed certain rituals and forms of personal devotion to contact their 'dead' mothers and fathers, sisters and brothers, grandmothers, etc. By contacting them, they could get to know the deeper truths about life and the spiritual path, deeper than they could attain by their own efforts. Through this contact with the ancestors they could obtain insights into the secrets of their future development, and also know the spiritual causes in which their day-to-day problems were rooted.

Ancient cultures were able to detect those places in nature where the veil dividing the two halves of humanity was easiest to transcend. There they created their burial mounds and stone circles to provide vehicles for successful communication between the two. In autumn 1998 I discovered such a place in the very west of Sweden, at Bohuslän. It is located on the island of Orust, and its name is Hoga.

The Hoga Center must have been in use from the Bronze Age up to the time of the Christian conversion, and during all that time it was making the connection between living people and their ancestors. Archaeological investigation shows different layers of time when the place was in use. It does not of course show why it was used or how. Those who used it have been taking part in the world of deceased for a long time now. So all that I could find out about the place's function was obtained by tuning in to their distant voices. Luckily, they have left behind in Hoga a double stone circle, a standing stone and earth works, and these helped me understand the ritual use of the place.

The ancient Hoga Center comprises two ritual paths which lead from opposite directions towards the double stone circle. This takes the form of an '8', symbol of eternity. On one side there is a plateau surrounded by earth mounds. According to my inner vision, this was a place of excarnation, i.e., a stripping of the flesh, where the body of the deceased was exposed to carnivorous birds. In the distance a standing stone marked the entrance to the underworld – though a later culture moved it to another place — and indicated the path that the soul should take to expose itself to the processes of purification and reintegration within the belly of the Mother Earth.

The next step on the deceased's path is indicated by the left-ward loop of the double stone circle. On the etheric plane, this place has been formed as a light bowl positioned just beneath the ground, its edge marked by the standing stones of the circle. It represents the gate through which the soul, purified of its earthly garments and patterns, could ascend towards the realms of the universal spirit.

Another ritual path has been laid out from the opposite side of the Hoga landscape. This is for the living family members who would like to approach their ancestors and talk to them. This path starts on a small plateau which is overlighted by an angelic being, and therefore a place where one would attune to the higher purpose of one's visit. Then the path curves, to lead past three thresholds where the pilgrims had to stop and successively express their oneness with the world of spirit, the inner purpose for their visit, and shout their secret spiritual name. Only then could they pass the guardian of the place and proceed to the next stop on the ritual path. It is easy to recognize this as a place of the fire spirits.

Nowadays the spot is marked by a grove of tall larch trees. Since the fire spirits are still there and stimulating the place with their explosive powers, the larch trees, which otherwise always tend to grow up straight, have grown in curious ways. Many of their trunks lean to one side or another, or even are curved. This is the place where the pilgrims — just for the duration of their contact with the deceased — would be deprived of the power to govern their physical body, so that they could experience themselves as a pure light presence. The elemental beings of fire are masters of such transformations, as I described in Chapter Two when I related my experience on Meissner mountain in Germany.

Only then were the pilgrims ready to enter the right-hand loop of the double stone circle, and there they could begin to communicate with their ancestors, put their questions and seek the answers. With my inner eye I could see a mound of white light within the circle and around the 'mound' a revolving light spiral connecting heaven and earth. Obviously it is located there to facilitate the sensitive communication between the worlds of the living and the 'dead': or more precisely, communication between

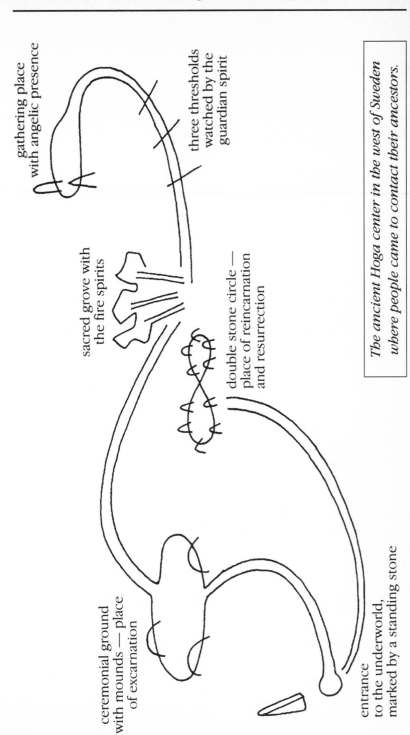

gathering place
with angelic presence

three thresholds
watched by the
guardian spirit

sacred grove with
the fire spirits

double stone circle —
place of reincarnation
and resurrection

ceremonial ground
with mounds — place
of excarnation

entrance
to the underworld,
marked by a standing stone

*The ancient Hoga center in the west of Sweden
where people came to contact their ancestors.*

those who are living right now in conditions of matter and those who are at this time living in the spirit.

When I see places like the Hoga Center, I am always surprised at how well they are maintained. They have been kept alert by the forces of nature, the elemental beings, and presumably also by the deceased, so that their message has not been lost even though the sites have been neglected for centuries by the living portion of the human family. It is still possible, even today, to experience their message.

It seems that the dream centered around the forgotten lime tree stump, which represented the totality of the human family, was given to make me aware that the world of the deceased wants to participate too in the process of forming the new earth cosmos. It seeks to assume once again the role in life that it ought to play. It does not belong only to the past but to the future too. Let us just realize that our future children will be chosen from among those same deceased souls in the 'world of shadow', to be among the people next born on earth.

We perceive the realm of the ancestors to be a world of shadow because we are in the habit of thinking of it as opposite to the 'the daylight world'. As a culture, we renege on any interest in the world of the dead beyond the formality of the funeral. Abiding in the half of the world which bathes in the physical light of the sun — perceived as positive — we assign to the world of the deceased a preconception of shadow and imbue it with the quality of negativity. And we tend not to talk about it.

During the last night of 1998 and only two nights after the first dream, I received another. This emphasized that behind our problem with the community of 'the dead' is concealed a deeper cultural problem which is draining the powers of our civilization. It is weakening us to such an extent that we cannot face the revelation of the new earth cosmos.

In my dream the room is dark, yet its features are perfectly visible because the moonlight is extremely bright. I notice a beautiful moth flying around me at hip height. I can feel the moth straining as it struggles to stay aloft. When I look closer, I see that her troubles are three-fold: her wings are loaded with small but heavy clumps of dust, and I feel as if I am being asked to relieve her of some of this extra weight; secondly, the wings have been wrapped in dusty spider webs. Both kinds of impediments can be understood as representing the false preconceptions and patterns of denial that our culture projects onto the 'shadowy' underworld, stripping it of its proper role in our everyday life.

Yet there is a third weight also hindering the moth's flight. Surprisingly, this has the form of a letter 'H', positioned over the whole width of its wings. I get the feeling that this is not an ordinary letter, but an 'H' such as is used in German spelling to denote a letter which is not spoken aloud. It is called 'the silent H'. I asked myself, what could it symbolize?

Since the moth had always been flying around my hips, I got the idea that it was pointing towards a blockage hidden deep within myself as representative of the human race. The symbol of 'the silent H' was to be sensed as denoting a quasi-totalitarian emotional pattern that is suppressing some quality within me and reducing it to absolute silence.

I was shocked, and for two weeks I did not know what to do about it. Then I had an intuition that I should go into meditation, but instead of focusing my attention on the heart center in my usual way, I should try to approach it from the back. I did so, and once again I was shocked.

Approaching the heart from its reverse side was like approaching the dark side of the moon. I felt there the coolness presented by moonlight, in contrast to the warmth of the sun's rays. It felt too like the deep scar of a never-healed wound, a 'waste land' with no traces of life.

At first I was upset when I realized that located within me there is a great part of myself which is frozen and consigned to oblivion. I tried to bathe the cold space behind my back with the warmth of my heart. But I soon realized that this was not the way to deal with my psyche's 'forbidden land'. Should I catch all the moths and turn them into butterflies? Should the moon be taken down from the sky because it cannot nourish life with warmth and energy?

I realized how one-sided was my constant preoccupation

with the sunny front-side of my being, furthering life processes and fostering the belief that death should come later — as much later as possible. Cradling my illusions, I do not realize that, while being alive, I am at the same time dead. Life is not a linear progress, but a synergetic unity in which life and death simultaneously take part.

In a practical sense, even though I am full of life right now, there is that other aspect of myself which I shall get to know fully only after I have died, though it is part of me in this moment too. As a member of a culture that concentrates so one-sidedly on the active face of life's reality, I am persistently blanking out that part of me which holds me rooted in eternity. It does not know activity, only the passivity of pure being. It is not interested in any particular expression of creation, but only in the wholeness of which light and darkness, time and eternity, earth and cosmos are a part. We used to call it the 'soul'.

But even though we know enough to call it the soul, in practice our cultural patterns demand that this aspect of our being should be closed up in the 'tower' space of our back. Yet the soul's purpose is not to remain locked up there, but to penetrate our whole being and imbue all our activities with the peace of infinity, together with the intuition that we are participants of eternity, all the time and with all that we are.

It is in this way that we should understand the apocalyptic image of death emerging from the grave of the underworld and taking over one quarter of the world. If a person's relationship 'upwards' to the spirit and 'downwards' to the earth represent two quarters of human reality, their relationship to the everyday life confronting them, i.e., in front of them, would represent the third quarter. The last quarter would then logically be represented by that shadowy space at the person's back, and thus belong to the 'powers of death' (i.e. the powers of the soul) within oneself.

The fourth apocalyptic rider, who appears in Revelation after the breaking of the fourth seal, is telling us that it will become impossible to keep the powers of eternity confined to the realms of the 'underworld' through the course of the earth changes and the accompanying transformation of the human race. They will take over the role that they play in the universe anyway. If human beings, enslaved by their cultural patterns, are unable to recognize that the powers of the world soul are part of life eternal and of their own essence, they will have to encounter them in the shape of the invincible powers of death.

Chapter Five

Hologrammic Touch — Exercises to Cope with the Earth Changes

We have been attempting to translate the language of the Seven Seals in the Revelation of St. John into the language of the recent earth changes. At this point I would like to take a break from this endeavor and instead ask what are we going to do about these changes. There is little sense in our knowing what is going on in the earth's transfiguration process without looking for ways to interact with it creatively. Once we know that a far-reaching change is about to transform our planetary home from within, we should ask ourselves, what can we do about it? We know that we are an indispensable part of the earth cosmos, so it is impossible that we should be excluded from the process.

Of course, one can say, "Let earth and nature transform themselves if that is what they have decided to do. Never mind, my body is part of them and so it will automatically change too." Yes, we are part of the earth cosmos and we cannot avoid changing if the life systems of earth undergo a process of transformation. But, as related to human beings, there is one special factor to be considered: our free will. If we do not consciously decide to change, we may stay stuck in the old patterns, even though the earth, for herself, has successfully blown them away.

This is why I decided to focus my attention initially on the phases of the change process that do not bother us very much at present because they are evolving on the invisible levels. If human beings do not change the co-related thought patterns, emotional attitudes and ways of behavior in time, we may one day find ourselves on one side of the abyss, while on the other side the earth has preceded us and is dancing on her path through eternal space.

These considerations lead us to the first exercise that should be practiced if we wish to attune to the changing earth.

Look at your thought patterns, emotional attitudes and ways of behaving

I am of course referring to the thought patterns, emotional attitudes and ways of behaving that relate to the earth, the nature kingdoms and our own being, which is also part of the earth cosmos. In writing this book, my intention is not just to entertain you with the story, however interesting, of the earth changes which are going on right now. I am also trying to provide you with a useful mirror composed of my experiences and insights. You may use this mirror to look at some of your own sensations and experiences, those which up till now you may not have been able to understand and fit into the pattern of your daily life. You may even have thrust such unusual experiences and feelings aside, trashing them under the label of personal problems. But after recognizing their true nature in a broader context, you can proceed to consciously change the underlying thought patterns, emotional attitudes and ways of behaving. Be creative with your experiences and your life!

Address a question to a tree or a shrub

When in the winter of 1998 I realized that the earth changes were under way, I was worried because I felt we were not ready to go along with them. So I sought to develop methods of attuning to the essence of the earth transformations, and for ways in which people could support them. But the subject was too new to me. I did not have enough experience of the new powers and qualities involved. Anyway, I was unable to discover any useful proposals out of my own resources.

To whom then could I go for help, if not to my own children? For many years they have collaborated with me in earth healing projects. So one day I asked my oldest daughter Ajra, who is married to Miska, to forget for a moment that she is a mother and a spiritual healer, and begin a discourse with her angel master in regard to my first experiences of the earth changes.

His answer placed the current changes in a broad context, which pleased me a lot because it confirmed my observations. At the end, we asked him if he could suggest some exercise that one could perform to attune to the earth changes.

He proposed that we should approach nature to get the right answers. Nature can never become separated from the essence of the earth. Therefore it offers us the best chance of attuning to what is happening with the earth at any given moment. The beings of nature know, beyond any illusion, how reality is vibrating at that moment and in what direction the earth is moving, taking with it the foundations of our life. This means that they can serve us as an accurate mirror to show where we may have got stuck in our own patterns, and so be losing our connection with the cycles of the changing earth..

The exercise should take the following pattern. Lovingly approach a tree or shrub, appreciating their beauty, and enter into inward communion with its presence. Then ask the being of the plant to demonstrate on your body where the problems are and what are their causes. Watch carefully for any feelings or intuitions that may arise afterwards, and pay attention to the part of the body to which your awareness is being led.

To illustrate what may occur, I am reminded of last autumn when I had inner problems and asked a group of beech trees on the Meissner Mountain about the causes of the difficulty. They directed my attention vertically downwards to the area of my knees, and then in a loop behind my back and upwards towards my head. There, instead of continuing with the circular movement, I bumped into a rigid area around my head. Only when I bowed my head down deep towards my heart chakra could the movement continue and be rounded off in a circle.

From this I understood that my mentality is dominating my world of feelings and intuition, and so blocking my natural tendency to flow with the course of the earth changes. I should connect my thought patterns more closely with the impulsive quality of my emotions. Then the obstacle would easily be overcome.

Hologrammic language and the cosmograms

By the beginning of 1999 I had finally got sufficiently clear about the course which the earth changes were taking to be able to develop ways of collaborating with them. It started with an inspiration that I received on February 11th, 1999. In a single electrifying moment I was struck by the idea that there ought to exist a language that could be understood by the consciousness of the Earth, by the spirits of nature, and by human and other cosmic beings as well. In the conditions of the unpredictable changes to come, we would all need a common language in which to communicate, mutually helping each other to overcome the difficulties which will doubtless arise in a process as complicated and long-enduring as this one may prove to be.

I was inspired to give the name of 'hologrammic touch' to the anticipated universal language. The word 'hologram' is composed of the Greek words 'holos' denoting the whole and 'gramma', which stands for the written letter. This corresponded exactly with my inspiration, that it should be 'a language written and understood by the whole of life'. But in our culture the word 'language' is too deeply associated with the linear flow of information to be used as a name for a different kind of communication that does not depend on the logical succession of impulses. To be able to be understood by beings that belong to other dimensions of intelligence, it should 'speak' beyond time, in other words, instantly.

This is why I started to associate the minutest gesture of 'touching' something with the universal language that I was seeking. By 'touching', one understands that a close connection between two subjects is happening in the moment. So it happened that, in the very instant following after the inspiration, my mind was 'touched' by the name that the inspiration was obviously carrying with it: 'hologrammic touch'.

The idea was not new to me. I have been working towards a universal language for three decades. At first, it was a theme which repeated itself rhythmically in my art work. Yet it was not until the beginning of the eighties that my work on the universal language found a practical application. I then started to develop

*Some of the cosmograms created by the author for his
lithopuncture project at Circuito das Aguas, Brazil, 1998.*

*Some of the cosmograms created by the author for his
lithopuncture project in Aachen, Germany, 1999.*

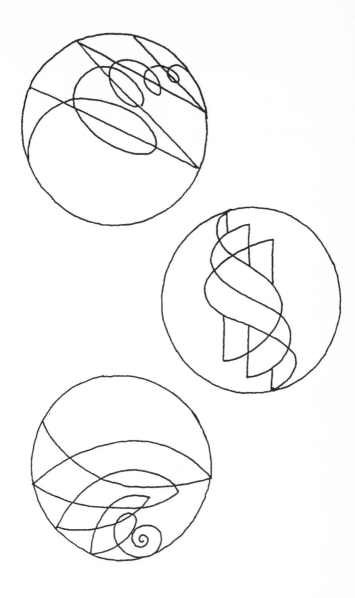

*Some of the cosmograms created by the author
for his lithopuncture project in the Seeland countryside
near Bern, Switzerland, 1999.*

Some of the cosmograms created by the author for his lithopuncture project on the both sides of the government border between Austria and Slovenia, 1999.

the language of the signs that I call 'cosmograms'. They became an indispensable part of my Earth healing work. I carve them on lithopuncture pillars that are subsequently positioned in the landscape. Sometimes I cast them in bronze so that they take the form of acupuncture plates, which I then install on the acupuncture points of a selected spot[1]. Sometimes, where the ambience is distorted, I even draw them in the ground so that the group working on healing the place can walk for a while along the lines of the cosmogram, in order to imprint it into the memory of the place.

At first glance, cosmograms look like the common sort of symbol, made up of lines and figures composed to convey a certain message. Simply look at the heritage of any culture and you will find a wealth of symbolic images which can be thought of as cosmograms. But true cosmograms have certain peculiarities which distinguish them from all other kinds of symbols. Primarily, they must be created in such a way that they are not just objective forms, but are imbued with their own consciousness. This means that they can address the viewer on a personal level — one could say a heart-to-heart level. They work on the basis of a mutual exchange between partners, and do not perform the mere function of transmitting information as do ordinary symbols.

To illustrate this, I will recount what happened last night when I started to write the portion of this book that you have just now been reading. I could not get absolutely clear about the essence of cosmograms, so I closed my computer down and went to sleep. Just before I got up to switch it on and start working again, I had a short dream which was obviously my inner self trying to help me tell the story of cosmograms.

In my dream I saw a woman who had hung her washing up on a clothes-line at the edge of a field and was going back to her home. In that very same moment she heard her baby behind her, screaming and weeping and calling out for her. She turned round and saw that by mistake she had hung her baby on the line too, among all sorts of underwear. Upset to see her baby hanging there, she ran to embrace it. Now, imagine that the underwear represents ordinary symbols and the screaming baby a cosmogram.

---

1 See photos of cosmograms in *Healing the Heart of the Earth*, pages 161, 167, 199, 201 and 205.

So that they can mediate between consciousnesses, or between beings belonging to different levels of existence, the cosmograms must also be created in a way that transcends mere logical or aesthetic design. They can only come about through a process of dialogue between the subjects involved. If I am about to create a cosmogram to support the identity of a place, I try to get to know its different dimensions. But the delivery of a cosmogram also requires that I use the knowledge gained to develop an inner communion with the place. Only in this way can the cosmogram arrive at its necessary multi-dimensional form[2].

To give another example of how a cosmogram can be created, I will talk about one I created yesterday while writing the present book, to protect myself from the unpleasant radiation emanating from my computer. I have written seven books in German during the past decade, and during that time enjoyed using pencil and eraser as my only tools. My editor then turned the text into computer language. This time, for the book you are now reading, I have been faced with the challenge of writing it in English and delivering it on a computer disc.

A month ago, soon after starting to write it on the computer, I began to feel a severe pain in my right arm and shoulder, which are the places most exposed to the computer screen. Since I usually work out of doors, I may be especially sensitive to this kind of radiation. At first I believed that my problems were due to some feelings of hesitation I was experiencing in the continuing process of my inner growth, and transcending the psychic patterns which, spiritually, I had outgrown. In fact, parallel with working on the book, I was also working busily on myself. Still, the pain didn't disappear. It was so severe that often I could not sleep.

In the meanwhile, I had started to get friendly with my computer, acknowledging it as a form of earth intelligence working through the crystals of silica on which its cybernetics are based. So it came about that the day before yesterday, while I was working on an earlier portion of this chapter, the computer screen suddenly showed a flash of crystal white light streaking diagonally across from its lower right to its upper left hand corner. The flash

2 There is more about the essence of cosmograms in *Healing the Heart of the Earth*, p. 159 and following.

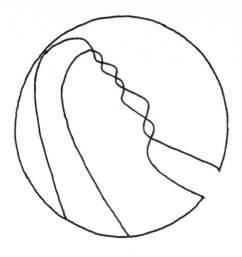

*The natural intelligence 'sitting' behind the computer
had told me how to create a cosmogram
which would protect me from the screen's radiation.*

had an undulating form. A few seconds later the phenomenon re-appeared. That was the end of it, and nothing more like this happened afterwards. But the light of the unexpected flash had been so strong that for the next few minutes I saw violet spots from of its imprint on my retina.

When I woke up yesterday morning, January 12th, 2000, I suddenly understood that the natural intelligence 'sitting' behind the computer had told me how to create a cosmogram which would protect me from the screen's radiation, to which I am obviously allergic. I immediately took a piece of paper and drew the two undulating lines which the computer had shown were the key to the problem. I also bent them backwards so that when I attached the paper to my right arm, which was the one that was hurting, they would point towards the screen. Their message was, "Always take back into yourself the kind of radiation that is coming out of you and hurting me!"

Before starting work, I attached the cosmogram to my arm with a safety pin, and in the course of working I have now and then telepathically reminded the computer intelligence to pay attention to the sign. It is now a day later and 10:25 AM. The pain has almost disappeared. I am sure that in a few days time I can let the sign go, because the computer will remember its message.

While I was engaged with cosmograms in the 'eighties, I discovered that the consciousness of the earth itself also uses the language of cosmograms to talk to the human race. The latest examples are the so-called crop circles that first appeared in England, but during the last decade have been the objects of admiration in a number of different countries. The crop circles come about through a lightning-fast interior biological process which bends the grain stalks so completely that they are laid in regular fashion next to each other on the ground. This process forms a cosmogram which can easily be read from the stalks which remain standing.

Also, while I was writing my book Christ Power and the Earth Goddess and studying the words of the Christ in the four Gospels, I discovered cosmograms imprinted in the ethers behind the layer of his teachings. Obviously, while he was talking to the minds of his contemporaries, he was simultaneously addressing their hearts through a hologrammic language. Ancient languages, like the Aramaic he was speaking, bear within their multi-dimensional tissue the natural ability to convey such a complex kind of message[3].

Hologrammic exercises

With the initiation of the earth changes, I felt the urge to 'translate' the knowledge derived from using cosmograms into a form that could be implemented in one's daily spiritual practice. Especially after January 1999, when I started to perceive the 'new energies' and their enormous power, I became aware that people will eventually get 'burned' if methods are not provided in time for them to attune to the illogical patterns of the energies and

---

3 See the Chapter entitled 'The Invisible Archetypal Pattern of the Gospels' in my book *Christ Power and the Earth Goddess*.

their archetypal quality. If these energies are not to work destructively but instead become the welcome helpers of change, they must be introduced into our personal power systems and invited to do their task within our individual and collective transformation processes.

However, I did not find a way to bring the inspiration of hologrammic touch into a practical form until February of the same year when, with my daughter Ana, we visited the island of Crete in the eastern Mediterranean. We had been invited there to conduct a one-week workshop which included practical work in earth healing in the country-side of Mesara, which is the central plain on the south side of the island.

While studying mythology and artifacts from the ancient Minoan culture that flourished in Bronze Age Crete, I discovered that they must have known the secret of the basic nourishing system of the earth. The use of its powers in ritual and daily life made it possible for Minoan culture to flourish in a state of balance and happiness for a millennium, while neighboring cultures were already trapped in the shackles of the patriarchal fight for power and dominance.

It was by observing clay figurines found in the ruins of the Minoan palaces in Knossos and Phaistos that I discovered the first three of the hologrammic exercises. My original thought had been to propose that the workshop group simply imitate the gestures portrayed by the figurines. But my intuition was telling me that the gestures by themselves do not penetrate deeply enough to invoke the archetypal powers of the nourishing system of the earth. More power was needed. It is the power of imagination that constitutes the spiritual identity of the human being. The divine ability to create, which is our natural heritage, would be useless if not accompanied by the appropriate creative tool. That tool is the power of imagination. This is the first reason why the gestures must be complemented with corresponding images forged in the imagination.

Furthermore, to be in tune with the emotional and spiritual levels of the earth changes, the imagination needs to work towards overcoming the patterns of division. Instead of losing ourselves in dualities, we need to strive to connect the opposites in all situations: in the case in point, between the earthly elements and their cosmic counterparts. This is the second reason why the hologrammic touch exercises will not attain their goal if the physical gestures — representing the powers of the earth — are not combined with the powers of imagination — representing the cosmos.

Let us now test the three exercises which I learned from the Minoan culture of Crete. They are good for starters because they help connect one's holon in all three directions: up and down, left and right, and forward and backward.

Exercise one (connecting up and down, see drawing)

1. Squat (knees-bend) to make yourself a symbol of the cosmos coming closer to the earth. Find a position that is comfortable enough for you to remain in it.

2. Raise your hands so that your palms are level with your throat as a symbol of the earth moving closer to the cosmos. Your elbows are half-flexed and extend a little to either side.

3. Then imagine that your hands and knees are holding a pillar of white light which reaches deep into the earth and high up towards the cosmos. Let the powers of the cosmos descend and the powers of the earth ascend simultaneously through the pillar.

4. Remain for a while like this and hold the image in your imagination.

Exercise two (connecting left and right, see drawing)

1. Stand or sit upright. Put your right hand on your left shoulder and your left hand on your right hip. At the same time, imagine that you are securing your powers in the very center of yourself, twisting them like a screw.

2. After a short while reverse your hands, so the left hand goes to the right shoulder and the right hand to the left hip, and then imagine that you are securing your powers by twisting in the other direction.

3. For a period of time, repeat changing the position of your hands and, in your imagination, the direction of twist.

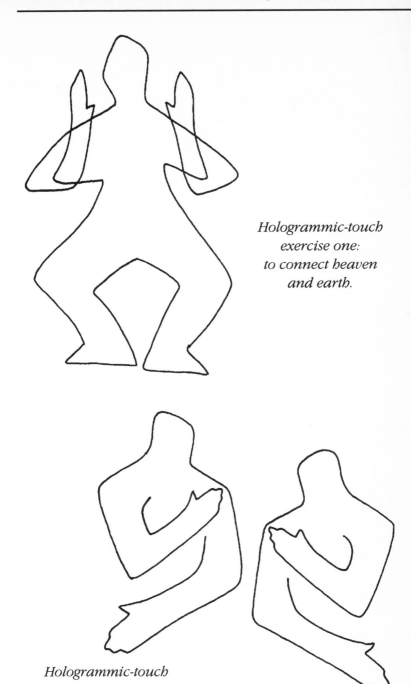

*Hologrammic-touch
exercise one:
to connect heaven
and earth.*

*Hologrammic-touch
exercise two:
to connect left and right.*

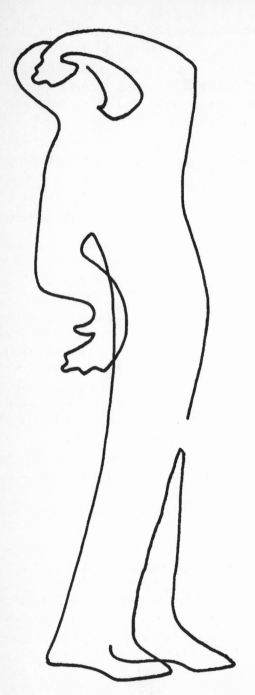

*Hologrammic-touch
exercise three:
to connect light and
shadow.*

Exercise three (connecting forward and backward, see drawing)

1. Place your right hand against your right hip with the palm turned backwards. This enables you to connect with the powers of the back. Imagine that you are holding something round and cold like a snowball in that hand.

2. Place your left hand on the center of your forehead with the palm held open towards your front and imagine it is holding something warm and shiny, like a small replica of the solar disc.

3. Take care to connect simultaneously with the warmth of the light and the coldness of the shadow, and continue holding both.

Do all three exercises one after another, because they represent a cycle.

I was shown the next two exercises by elemental beings on Meissner, the sacred mountain, where I was communicating with the spirits of water and fire as described in Chapter Two. I went up a path to the top of the rock within which the beings of fire have their focus, and then came to the realm of the beings who belong to the Air Element. My sight was opened to the kingdom of the fairies. But the meeting soon ceased to be merely enjoyable, because the whole crowd of beautiful beings closed in as if they were threatening me and about to press against the fringe of my aura. I had the intuition that they had something to communicate to me.

As soon as I allowed my body to follow my intuition, my hands started to move, obviously motivated by the fairies to demonstrate some kind of exercise. Their accompanying message — translated into logical concepts — said that people in general always keep their hearts nearly closed, and share love only among themselves. As a result, there is a lack of love in the air. This is a particular problem for the fairy folk because it is primarily from the power of love that they can 'knit' a joyous and uplifting psychic atmosphere for each locality. They simply cannot do it properly any more. People, like all other beings, are expected to give out the power of their hearts in exchange for the power of life they receive from nature. We have the ability to be a 'cosmic love-creating machine' — this is what I understood them to say — but we are caught in our ego-centric rut, and hold back the flow of love.

The following exercise would help them and ourselves as well:

Exercise four (help for elemental beings, see drawing)

1. Put your hands in front of your heart so that only the middle fingers are touching and your hands are forming a kind of barrier. Then, for a little while, enhance and concentrate the powers of love emanating from your heart behind the barrier.

2. Then open the barrier by extending your arms to stretch diagonally upwards, with your hands open and giving, and imagine the streams of love flowing into the environment.

3. Repeat the exercise a few times, feeling love for the nature around you.

I had been teaching groups this exercise for a couple of months, when, while practicing it with a group in Basle, Switzerland, the Earth Soul suddenly appeared in front of me and asked me to use a preamble. Its purpose is to connect with the powers of the elemental being within us before we send out our impulses. This is the preamble She showed me: Lower your hands — the middle fingers touching — down to the level of your sex and connect with the elemental powers within you. Then raise your hands slowly up to the level of your heart. With the middle fingers still touching, hold them in the shape of a bowl in front of your heart, and imagine that your elemental powers are connecting with the heart quality (see drawing). Only then should you start doing the above exercise, repeating It a few times. The preamble should be done only once, at the beginning.

Going back to the event on Meissner, I was immediately taught another hologrammic exercise. As if attracted by my having learnt to open my heart to nature, a mighty being approached me from behind. It must have been a highly evolved guardian of

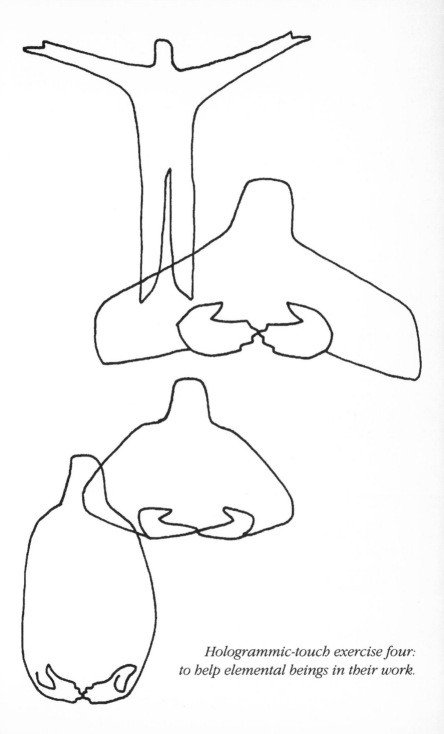

Hologrammic-touch exercise four:
to help elemental beings in their work.

Hologrammic-touch exercise five:
for rounding off the space.

nature called a 'deva'[4]. I turned around and, without need of any words, understood that I was being offered the opportunity to learn an exercise which would help nature spirits and elemental beings in their new work of transforming the face of the earth.

The explanation accompanying the exercise told me that one of the main challenges which face the forces of nature in their work is the linear structuring of the 'world crust' that is maintained and nourished by the thought patterns of our civilization. It is in dramatic opposition to the balanced, rounded and holistic organism of the earth cosmos that the elemental world is trying to re-establish during the course of the present earth changes. By doing the proposed exercise, people could help the elementals in their endeavor to overcome the blockages imposed by the collective human mind.

Exercise five (rounding off the ambience, see drawing)

1. With one hand link to the cosmic realms above, and with the other hand link to the earthly realm below.

2. While holding your hands one above the other, imagine that you are holding a fine membrane composed of rainbow colors upright between them. The membrane is so large that it reaches out in a bow to the furthest horizon of the ambience where you are standing. By ambience is meant not only the space above, but also below, in the earth. In consequence, the membrane has a circular shape, one half of it rising high above the ground, the other delving deep down into the earth.

3. Then, very slowly and using absolute care, turn to the right. While you are turning around, carry the rainbow membrane with you so that the ambience above and below the ground has to pass through it. Use your imagination to make sure that this 'passing through' is being accomplished in each moment that you are turning around. The exercise is completed when you have gone through the whole 360 degree circle. If you want, you can repeat it once more by turning in the opposite direction.

---

4 See *To Hear the Angels Sing* by Dorothy McLean and *The Findhorn Garden* written by the Findhorn Community.

I have already mentioned my work in the landscape around Dachau, Germany, site of the infamous Nazi concentration camp. While working there on healing the place's energetic and emotional wounds, its spirit showed me another exercise which connects heaven and earth within us and around us. Interestingly, in doing this exercise, one uses one's hands to 'draw' the symbol called the 'Star of David'. This is the Jewish symbol for the sacred marriage between heaven and earth, but it is also the symbol which the majority of prisoners had to wear on their clothing to show that they belonged to the Jewish race, which the Nazis intended to extinguish.

Exercise six (the Star of David, see drawing)

1. Raise your hands above your head so as to form a kind of a pyramid, and through its peak connect with the cosmic powers above.

2. Lower your hands slowly, stretching them out diagonally, and let the accumulated momentum of the cosmic powers flow into the earth.

3. Then let your hands form a downward pointing triangle to connect with the earthly powers.

4. Raise your hands slowly upwards, stretching them out diagonally, and let the gathered momentum of the earthly powers flow towards the universe.

5. Then form the triangle above your head to connect once again to the cosmic powers... and continue repeating the exercise at least ten times.

After the 'Star of David' exercise had been revealed to me in Dachau, it became usual for the places where I was doing earth healing work to reveal the cosmogram of their identity by showing me a new hologrammic exercise. The landscape of the Sumava region of Bohemia (called Sudeten in German) went through the trials of severe ethnic cleansing twice during the Second World War. First during Nazi rule, all the Czech people were expelled from their homes. Then, when the communist troops took over, the same thing happened to the German majority. While I was working there to heal the traumas of the land with an international group of people from Holland and Bohemia and we had gone to a place called Humpolec, the soul of the region showed me her variation of the hologram for connecting heaven and earth:

Exercise seven (Humpolec exercise, see drawing)

1. Use all your strength to stretch your arms down beside your body. Then concentrate the earth powers within you by tightly clenching your fists. Do this three times and imagine that you are pumping the earth powers into your body.

2. Then raise your arms straight out to either side with the palms of your hands held open and facing down, and continue raising them so that they trace a circle around your body till they point straight upwards to form a channel above your head. To form the channel the hands should be held apart but positioned back to back. Imagine for a while that cosmic powers are streaming into your body through this channel.

3. Then bring your hands down, tracing the same circle in reverse, and imagine that you are gathering together and merging the earthly and cosmic powers within your heart.

4. In this way you return to position 1, and start again. Repeat the exercise for as long as it feels right for you to do so.

While working on earth healing with a group of like-minded people in Basle, Switzerland, the place showed me another variation on the exercise for connecting the light and the dark sides within the human being. This was done through the medium of a sculpture of a strong woman, who represents the soul of Basle, taking care of children. This monument was donated to Basle by the French government in gratitude for the city's care of French refugees during the second world war. Characteristically, this 'Goddess sculpture' is positioned just beside the vital powers' Yin-center in the Basle landscape. This center is located at the fringe of the Schützenmatt Park.

Exercise eight (to connect the basic powers of the back with the solar powers of the front, see drawing)

1. Stretch your hands behind you so that your middle fingers touch each other just above your buttocks. Connect with the basic powers of the earth.

2. Move your hands so that they glide up along your body till they stretch out diagonally above you. Bring them together there so that the middle fingers touch again, palms facing down.

3. While your hands are gliding upwards, you should lean your head back as much as possible so that the throat chakra becomes exposed.

4. While holding your head back and middle fingers touching, imagine that you are concentrating the basic powers of the back in your throat chakra to become the creative powers of the Word.

5. Then with open hands stretch out your arms so that the powers of the Word can flow freely into the world.

6. Bring your hands down and straighten your neck, to start again from the beginning...

While working in Bosnia in July 1999, my group visited a necropolis built by the Bogumil culture in the Middle Ages. Like the Cathars in France, the Bogumils were rebelling against the patriarchal power of the dominant Christian church, which treated them as a dangerous sect[5]. Bogumils are known to have developed a strong cult of the dead, composing their necropolises from blocks of stone engraved with highly interesting symbols. While we were tuning into such a necropolis at Radmilja, the ancestors inspired me to discover a hologrammic gesture meaning, "The Christ is within". This refers to the central belief of the Bogumil movement, that the divine is not to be sought in rituals and other expressions of devotion, but within one's own being.

---

5 For a good book on the Bogumils, see *Die Bogumilen* by Rudolf Kutzli, Verlag Urachhaus, Stuttgart, 1977.

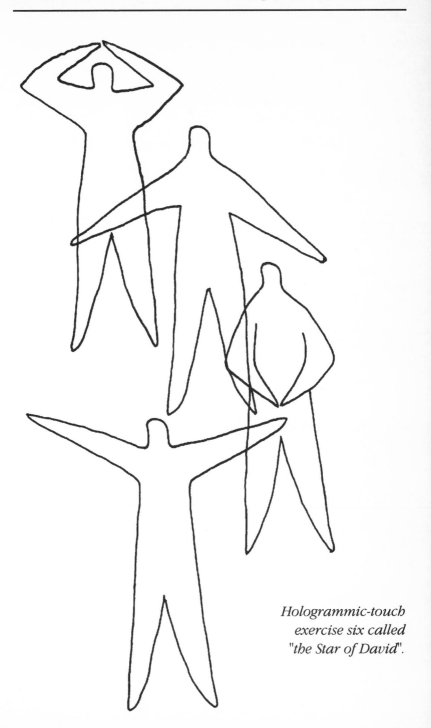

*Hologrammic-touch
exercise six called
"the Star of David".*

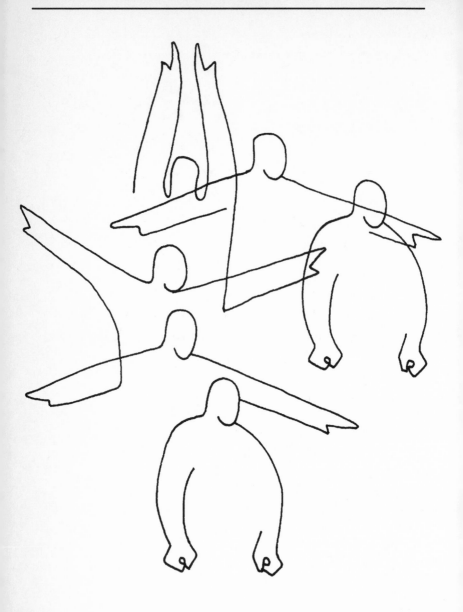

Hologrammic-touch exercise seven:
to connect earth and heaven.

Hologrammic-touch exercise eight:
to connect the basic powers of the back
with the solar powers of the front.

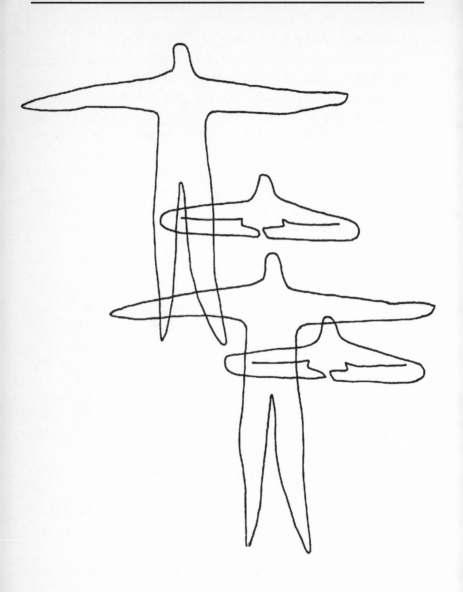

Hologrammic-touch exercise nine:
'divinity within'.

Exercise nine (Divinity within, see drawing)

1. Stretch out your hands horizontally so that you form a cross. Be part of the whole universe.

2. Then bend both hands back towards your body so that the palms gently touch the left and right sides of the middle portion of your chest. (If you wish you can say silently: The Christ is within.)

3. At the moment you touch your chest — where the two chakras relating to the Water Element are located — imagine that a stream of milky white light streams instantly down to the heart of the earth.

4. Repeat the gesture a few times.

When the hologrammic touch exercises were being revealed, I was shown several that can be done with just the two hands, without moving the whole body. These can be comfortably performed in constrained situations, such as when doing hologrammic exercises with people seated in a conference hall. Let me describe some of them here, starting with the one which has a specially strong relationship to the 'new powers'. It was shown me by the guardian spirits of the ancient sanctuary of Seesteine on Meissner Mountain in Germany.

Exercise ten ('The grinding millstones of love', see drawing)

1. Place one hand above the other in front of your chest and imagine that, as in the yin-yang sign, one hand is touching light (the white field), and the other darkness (the black field).

2. Then move your hands so that one edge glides all around the edge of the other. The edges of your hands should touch like millstones all the time you are turning them around.

3. After a while imagine that you take the 'grinding millstones' into the space of your heart and continue with the 'milling' there.

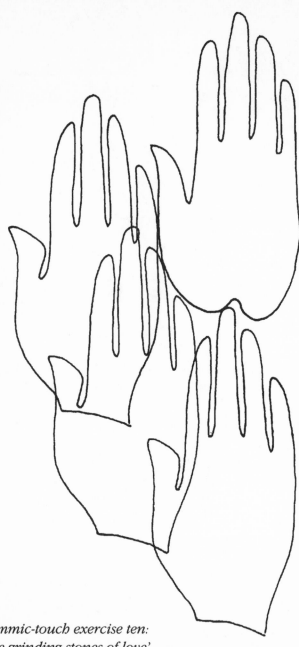

Hologrammic-touch exercise ten:
called 'the grinding stones of love'.

*Hologrammic-touch
exercise eleven:
to experience the
integrity of the heart.*

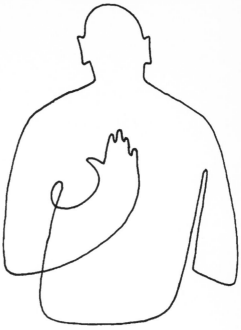

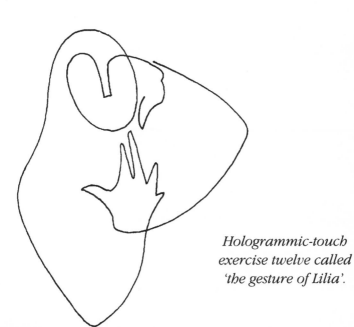

*Hologrammic-touch
exercise twelve called
'the gesture of Lilia'.*

Exercise eleven (Experiencing the integrity of the heart, see drawing)

1. Place one hand on your back (back of the hand to your back!), positioning it behind the heart chakra. It represents the dark aspect of the heart powers.

2. Place the other hand successively on your belly, on your throat and finally on the center of your chest. Each time connect with the hand behind your back, and remain in each position for a while. In this way you make sure that all three aspects of the heart chakra, emotional, mental and spiritual, are connected to its source which is beyond anything.

While I was visiting Turku, Finland, to prepare a lithopuncture project for the city, I got to know the sculptures of the local 20th century sculptor Wäinö Aaltonen. I was amazed at how much he knew about the language of gestures. I should like to mention the gesture portrayed in his beautiful sculpture of a woman called 'Lilia'[6].

Exercise twelve (The gesture of Lilia, see drawing)

1. Touch the little hollow below your throat with the index and middle finger of one hand.

2. Place the fingers of the other hand in the hair behind your neck.

3. After a short while let your imagination follow in the direction indicated, backwards from the throat, to enter the realms of your soul.

Here are two more hologrammic gestures that I discovered during my extensive travels in the summer of 1999:

---

6 Rudolf Steiner's inspiration leading to the development of Eurhythmy represents another excellent research project which points in the direction of the universal language.

Exercise thirteen (Connecting with the ancestors, see drawing)

1. Bring both hands down to the level of your sex, one with the palm upwards, the other downwards.

2. Connect both middle fingers firmly and then move gently with your imagination into the presence of the underworld[7].

Exercise fourteen (A grounding exercise, see drawing)

1. Place both hands in front of your heart so that the fingers of one hand are pointing upwards and the others downwards. Only the tips of the thumbs are touching each other.

2. Imagine that the four fingers that are pointing downwards are extending in the form of light rays, penetrating deep down into the earth. Simultaneously the fingers of the other hand, pointing upwards, are extending as light rays high up into the universe to touch the stars. Remain for a while like this, anchored in the earth and the heavens.

3. Then clench the four fingers of both hands so that the light rays disappear. You concentrate on the point where both thumbs are touching each other. This represents your heart center where the earthly and cosmic powers are intertwined.

4. Remain for a moment like this, then stretch your fingers out again...etc.

Exercise fifteen (The Manhattan Exercise)

As a last example, I would like to present an exercise that was shown me by the spirit of Manhattan during preparations for a workshop given by my daughter Ana and myself in November 1999 in Central Park, New York. In Chapter Four I mentioned how deeply the light-body of Manhattan Island is rooted in the depth of the earth. As such, the island is capable of carrying upon its shoulders the most head-oriented and yet most highly creative cultural layers. The exercise offers us exactly the same quality of grounding the mental activity while at the same time 'opening the head' to the breadths of eternity.

---

7 The Minoan double-headed ax is the corresponding visual symbol.

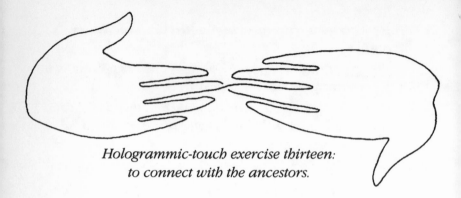

Hologrammic-touch exercise thirteen:
to connect with the ancestors.

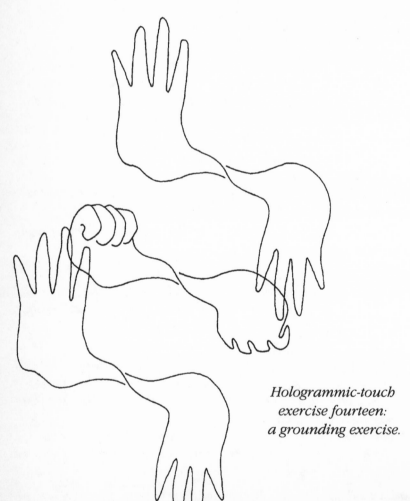

Hologrammic-touch
exercise fourteen:
a grounding exercise.

*Hologrammic-touch
exercise fifteen:
to ground the powers of the
mental upsurge.*

Exercise fifteen   (to ground the powers of the mental upsurge, see drawing)

1. You bow down towards the earth while imagining that your hands are going even deeper into the body of the earth.

2. Slowly drawing yourself up, you pull the connection with the earth up with you along your vertical axis. Place your hands together, pointing downward at the level of your sex, and then, pointing upward, at the level of your heart.

3. Continue raising your hands and when they reach the level of your face, stand still for a moment and, with your hands in front of your head, concentrate on the gesture of prayer.

4. After a while, start to slowly extend your hands out horizontally, reaching to the left and the right as far as you are able.

5. Bow down to the earth again and start from the beginning.

Chapter Six

Earth Changes — Personal Context, Cosmic Perspectives

Now that we become acquainted with some of the tools that we can use to engage ourselves personally and creatively in the process of change, we are sufficiently well equipped to open the fifth of the Apocalypse's Seven Seals. This one speaks of the transformation of the human being on all levels of existence. No power can force this complicated process upon us because we have a human right to freely decide whether or not we shall be open to transformation. The heavenly forces will have to be patient and continue offering people more and more opportunities to entice them to go a step further and submit to the need to change.

There is really no more information supplied by the symbolic text attached to the story of the Fifth Seal. It speaks of human souls who were ready to put on white garments and of those who were not yet ready. In the language of symbols, wearing white garments means that the person is going through the transforming process of an initiation. Some are already clothed, but then a heavenly voice told them "to be patient a little longer, until the number of their fellow-servants and of their brethren, who were to die as they had died, should be complete." (Rev 6:11) The dying can of course also be understood symbolically. To die to the old denotes that one is ready to be born to the new.

My counselor from the elemental world, with whom I was elaborating on the phases of the earth changes and the related personal transformations, advised me to look in the Seven Letters to the Seven Churches in Asia Minor for more information.

He was obviously referring to that rather boring, initial portion of the Revelation of St. John which I usually skipped in order to arrive sooner at the parts of the text which interested me more. The Letters contain instructions on how the early Christian congregations should face the problems posed by certain sects, the proper moral attitude of a Christian believer, etc. But why should we bother ourselves today with the difficulties faced by the early Christian Churches in the first century AD?

It is true that the Seven Letters addressed to the Churches in Ephesus, Smyrna, Pergamon, Thyatira, Sardis, Philadelphia and Laodicea speak mainly about the local problems of that distant era. But this is a concern not only of this particular portion of Revelation, but to some extent it affects the whole text. It is easy to get lost in the old and outgrown dualistic patterns which appear again and again throughout the whole Apocalypse.

If we let those outgrown patterns guide us throughout the text, then, without exaggeration, Revelation could be read in the following way. At its beginning, the Seven Letters tell us the rules to be obeyed by a faithful follower of the Christ. Those who do obey receive a divine stamp on their foreheads. Those who do not, get the stamp of evil. Later on, the divine Judge will appear on the throne and divide those who wear the divine stamp from those who have been stamped with the mark of evil. The first ones go to the heavenly New Jerusalem, the second ones to Hell.

This pattern is no fantasy of mine. It is a story that can be extracted from the text itself. I believe that this is the primary way in which the Apocalypse has been explained for centuries. I am no longer angry at this horrific pattern which segregates and divides the human family into good and bad halves[1]. I have even come to think that it has performed a positive function, by weaving a cloak of illusion which has hidden the true knowledge of the future evolution of the earth and of humanity. Thus the Apocalypse could safely convey this knowledge down to the present time when we desperately need it.

When we study the Apocalypse, we must remember that we

---

1 For more on the dangers inherent in the dualistic pattern of thought, see my book Christ Power and the Earth Goddess, Chapter 8.

have to do with a multidimensional text. Its outer layers may be banal and outgrown, but there are other levels that even nowadays may be too novel for our understanding. My approach is to use my intuition to inwardly feel out those portions of the text that belong to the layer which has been hidden, so as to appear in our consciousness during the present epoch[2]. Then I meditate on the message that seeks to be revealed through the words in front of me.

Let us take as an example the first of the Apocalyptic letters, the Letter to the Church in Ephesus. My intuition tells me to put aside all other portions of the text spoken by the divine voice, and take only the following: "I know what you have done; I know how hard you have worked and what you have endured...But I hold this against you, that you do not love as you did at first." (Rev 2:2) I consider these words to be a message relevant to our theme. But I must confess that I do not fully trust the phrase, "...love as you did at first". Other translations which talk about "forgetting the primeval love" feel more accurate.

Let me try to put the message in words we can understand. Human beings are fantastic doers. We are able to work hard and create incredible buildings and cities, and even fight persistently for truth, or for human rights, or the safety of the environment. We are able to use our hands and minds in the most surprising ways. But all these fantastic creations are of little worth and relegated to oblivion if we do not know how to manifest them through love.

The expressions, 'first love' and 'primeval love' signify that the text does not mean love in any one of its particular facets, such as emotional love, love for one's neighbor, sexual love etc. It means love in its totality as a cosmic power that connects everything with anything in the universe. It is the power of the heart that knows of no division but is equally loving towards the light and the dark, the good and the evil, the earthly expressions of life and the heavenly ones...To manifest through love means to affiliate

---

2 The multidimensionality of Revelation is so potent that each epoch can find a different kind of message within its layers. Each message is the one most appropriate for that epoch. For an example of this versatility, see the 12 lectures on the Apocalypse given by Rudolf Steiner in Nuremberg in 1908.

one's creation with the waves of eternity, while it simultaneously shows itself in practical action. It means bringing joy to the whole of creation, while taking care of a single particle of its weaving.

The Letters to the Seven Churches are composed in such a way that the reader is first advised which quality must be furthered in one's personal daily spiritual practice in order to stay in tune with the progress of the epochal changes which we are witnessing in and around us. But then, in their last sentence, the Letters formulate the 'reward' that the person will achieve if they persistently endeavor to embody the prescribed quality in their life. In this way, the present task is complemented by the future goal.

In the Letter to Ephesus the human being's reward is declared to be the divine gift of becoming able to embody simultaneously the infinite character of eternity as well as the exclusivity of the time-and-space dimension. In the words of the Letter, "To the victorious I will give the right to eat from the tree of (eternal) life which grows in the paradise of God."

The key sentence from the second Letter, the one addressed to the Angel of Smyrna says: "Have no fear of what you will suffer." (Rev 2:10) If we try to conceptualize for ourselves all the upheavals that must happen to the earth and to our being before the earth cosmos can be ordered in a new way, we can imagine that there will be much to be afraid of. Just think of the masses of people who are attached to the present static version of earth. To shake them out of that attachment, the earth may have to make dramatic changes which upset the emotional, energetic and physical levels. Then people may easily get in a panic and give way to fears of every kind.

The Letter to Smyrna would persuade us to accept troubles as a normal ingredient of the change process, to take them as a creative challenge and a chance to progress on our personal path of transmutation. In any dramatic situation that may arise, we should know that the process of epochal change has been perfectly guaranteed in advance. This is true for the earth cosmos as well as for the human evolution There is no need at all for us to nurture fears. A massive explosion of fear could rather threaten the victorious outcome of the changes. To be inwardly at peace, no matter how upsetting our surrounding circumstances, is the attitude that the second Letter demands from each one of us. Hold fast to the inner peace at each moment, no matter how dramatic the situation.

And what does the Letter offer in exchange? "The victorious cannot suffer the slightest hurt from the second death." What does this mean in practice? The "first death" symbolizes the normal death of the physical body and the soul's transcendence to the etheric level of existence. Following this logic, the second death would denote a much more fatal retrogression on the personal spiritual path, one which could symbolically be understood as the 'death of the soul'. But since the soul belongs to the shoreless sea of eternity, it can never die.

In ancient times the symbol of the 'second death' was more representative of a serious retrogression on the personal evolutionary path, with the threat that one might lose one's personal identity. So there is an obvious correspondence between submitting to one's fears and losing one's sense of identity. Contrary wise, holding to one's inner peace secures one's personal advancement on the path of individuation, till we become who we really are.

In the third Letter, addressed to the Angel of the Pergamon Church, the key quality put forward is expressed in a single imperative, 'Convert!'[3] The note sounded by this word demands — in the sharpest way — that we get personally in tune with the times of change. We are advised to use the opportunity they offer to watch constantly for what next needs changing within our psychic world, spiritual attitudes, personal relationships etc. These times enable changes to be accomplished quickly and with relative ease. But if you neglect the opportunities for change, one after another, you can expect to be submerged in severe problems. And they may help the changes to happen, finally.

Those who persevere in walking the path of change can reach the goal described in the divine words: "I will give the victorious...a white stone with a new name written upon it which no man knows except the man who receives it." (Rev 2:17) This is a

---

3 In comparing this text with other translations, I consider the translation I have used up to now to be inaccurate at this point. It translates the imperative as "Repent!" Instead, I prefer "Convert!'

promise that one can reach a more advanced level of identity, one which vibrates beyond the egocentric self which characterizes the modern human being.

The key words of the fourth Letter, the one written for the Angel of Thyatira, are hidden within the phrase spoken by the divine voice, "Know that I am the one who searches men's hearts and minds." It urges everybody to renounce the cherished illusions and devices which people use to deceive others about themselves. Till now, for example, it was possible to keep traumas, resentments or even hate-filled emotions deeply hidden within one's psyche and still function perfectly well on a social level. This is no longer the case. In the course of the earth changes we will find more and more frequently that a person's hidden motives or covert illusions will surface instantly to become evident to everybody. It is simply the way that the powers of change work.

The wise will learn to have no hesitation in avoiding dual personality ploys. Be faithful to the person you really are, in any situation and at any time. Only then will we be rewarded with the promise given to the Angel of Thyatira: "To the one who is victorious, who carries out my work to the end, I will give authority over the nations, just as I myself have received authority from my Father, and I will give him the morning star." (Rev 2:26) The 'morning star' is another name for Venus, the star of the Goddess. The goal of the Angel of Thyatira is to lead each individual beyond illusion and towards the revelation of her or his inner Goddess and the God-Within. The first aspect of our divine origin is symbolized by Venus, the second by the 'authority over the nations'.

The Letter to Sardis starts with the clear words, "Write this to the Angel of the Church in Sardis: These are the words of him who holds in his hand the seven Spirits of God and the seven stars: I know... that you have a reputation for being alive, but that in fact you are dead." (Rev 3:1) This letter addresses a theme we already know: the unavoidable reintegration of the dark aspects of life into the totality of life and the cosmos.

A peculiar dream, received on October 5th, 1998, had made me aware of this theme which has been brought to the fore by the progress of the earth changes. I had dreamed that in passing my neighbor's courtyard, I saw my white rabbit there, jumping around. I mustered my courage, knocked at my neighbor's door and demanded that the rabbit be given back to me. Without hesitation the man disappeared for a moment and came back holding a rabbit which was gray in color. He tried to persuade me that this was my animal. I persisted that mine was completely white. My neighbor disappeared again and came back with a white rabbit. I was relieved because I was sure that I was getting my rabbit back. I took it home quite happily, even though I had noticed, at the moment it was being handed over, that hidden behind its hind leg was a black spot, which mine did not have.

It was a year before I had advanced sufficiently far in my understanding of the new constitution of the earth cosmos to be ready to listen to my inner voice commenting on the dream as follows: "The message of the dream is to emphasize the new relationship between the forces of light and the forces of darkness. They both represent legitimate aspects of life. It is not possible to celebrate one of them without automatically furthering the other. It is not possible to fight for the light without that, somewhere else, the dark counterpart is reinforced and animated. This is the universal law of balance, symbolized by the gray rabbit, which can no longer be ignored. Ways must be found to integrate the so-called dark forces, so that they can again become part of the whole."

On the personal level, this would mean seeking to detach oneself from the one-sided striving for the positive, for the light and the good, which ends in the illusion of peace sleeping on a pile of arms. This is the illusion symbolized by the white rabbit with the hidden black spot. In the Letter to Sardis this is signified by the contradiction that one seems to be alive and yet is dead. The Fifth Letter rather urges us to transcend the human preference to dwell exclusively on the surface of life — which we identify with light — and instead dive deeper into its inner secrets. The life eternal does not know anything that can be excluded from the cosmic whole without crippling it. The universal whole, based on the perfect balance between opposites, includes darkness as well as light.

"The victorious shall wear white garments, and never shall I erase his name from the book of life." (Rev 3:5) In regard to the divine vision towards which the human being is evolving, the

Letter to Sardis emphasizes the angelic facet of our origin. This is symbolized by the white garments and the eternal quality ascribed to the book of life. Beyond the long-enduring story of our incarnations, in our essence as human beings we are also a part of the world of spirit — in this case identified with the angelic world — and there we belong, finally to be reintegrated.

The key words addressed to the angel of the Church in Philadelphia are: "You have been faithful to my message and have not denied my name." (Rev 3:8) What is hidden behind this oracular statement? I have pondered again and again over its meaning, which speaks directly to the heart yet is difficult to translate into the rational language of everyday life. Quite often, when I have lectured on the Revelation of St. John, I have simply forgotten to mention the Letter to Philadelphia, perhaps seeking to avoid the collective trauma which is shared by people of our modern civilization and which also troubles me. My audience would then embarrass me by asking about the missing commentary.

Each of us has come to the earth with the intention that — besides working on our inner development – we will assist in the divine plan to restore the earth cosmos to its original beauty. What causes each one of us immense pain is our human society's compulsion, while we are still little children, to push us into the prescribed cultural patterns in such a way that we forget our promise. Usually, we completely forget our primary purpose for being alive in the here and now. This is perhaps the deepest pain which individually we carry in our subconscious, even if, as people, we are never ready to admit it.

Yet all that is asked of us is to have the courage to inwardly ask what changes are necessary in our attitude to our personal life and how to rededicate it to its spiritual purpose. Instead of being constantly tortured by a bad conscience, we should make the effort to hold to our role in the universal creation: "As for the victorious, I will make him a pillar in the Temple of my God, and he will never leave it. I will write upon him the name of my God, and the name of the city of my God, the New Jerusalem which comes down out of Heaven from my God. And I will write upon him my own name. Let the listener hear what the Spirit says to the Churches." (Rev 3:12)

Letter	The Key Words of its Message	The Future Goal
Ephesus	Do not forget the primeval love	To be eternal while being temporal
Smyrna	Have no fear (Hold fast to inner peace!)	Your advancement on the path of individuation is secured
Pergamon	Convert! (Accept the changes)	Get to know your essential identity
Thyatira	Search your heart and mind (No cheating!)	Get to know your inner Goddess/God presence
Sardis	You are alive and yet dead (Integrate light and dark!)	Get to know your angelic origin
Philadelphia	Remember your spiritual purpose!	You will take over your role in the universe
Laodicea	Be either cold or hot (Decide!)	You will become a co-creator with the Divinity.

The Seven Letters

Finally, we have arrived at the seventh Letter, the one addressed to the angel of the Laodicean Church. It is dedicated to the quality of freedom, a quality which is the unique privilege of the human being. Let us listen to the key words spoken by the divine voice: "I know...that you are neither cold nor hot. I could wish that you were either cold or hot! But since you are lukewarm and neither hot nor cold, I intend to spit you out of my mouth!" (Rev 3:15)

These are words of urgent warning. If people submissively follow the ruling patterns, cultural, psychological, political and so on, subduing their own decisions to the opinion of the mass media or to political, religious or other propaganda, they are neglecting the highest divine gift that they have inherited, the right to choose freely. The whole evolutionary cycle marked by our struggle to obtain the 'knowledge of good and evil' (remember Adam and Eve!) is then made purposeless. We are struggling to stand on our own feet and to have the ability to make decisions by listening to the intuition of our hearts and the reasoning of our minds. If we let other forces, political groups or impersonal patterns, decide for us, we run the danger of being led to nowhere.

Severe trials will face us in the era of change. We will have to choose between what is right for us and what is wrong according to the feelings of our heart and the reasonings of our mind – each in tune with the other. The Letter to Laodicea speaks symbolically of the choice between the opposites of cold and hot. If we are not ready to choose, we can get lost in illusions which are symbolized by the lukewarm quality. As a result of our incapacity to say a clear YES or NO in any given situation, and as a last chance to save our integrity, we could unexpectedly be 'spat out of life'. Beyond death, when one arrives in the realms of spirit, it is much easier to distinguish between the qualities of 'cold' and 'hot'.

If individuals should prove that they have learned to stand firm by the decisions of their hearts, they will be assigned their future role in the universal creation: "As for the victorious, I will give him the honor of sitting beside me on my throne, just as I myself won the victory and have taken my seat beside my Father on his throne." (Rev 3:21)

Thus far, the Seven Letters can help us understand the fifth phase of the earth changes, which has to do with the transformation of the human being. The next step is to listen to the opening of the Sixth Seal. We should not get in a panic when we listen to the text of the Sixth Seal, but remember that we are dealing with symbolic language: "While he broke the sixth seal there was a tremendous earthquake, the sun turned dark like coarse black cloth, and the full moon was red as blood. The stars of the sky fell upon the earth, just as a fig tree sheds unripe figs when shaken in a gale. The sky vanished as though it were a scroll being rolled up, and every mountain and island was jolted out of its place." (Rev 6:12)

We should remember that the messages of the first Four Seals were conveyed in another way, being presented by different Apocalyptic riders. Riders moving along on their horses without themselves touching the earth represent different forces involved in the earth changes. The first four phases of the earth changes are evolving on the invisible levels. The fifth one is related to changes within the human being. It is obvious that the text of the Sixth Seal refers to changes on the physical level of the planet. It touches the level of existence about which people are most sensitive.

The earthquake is a generalized symbol of a change in the earth's surface. After an earthquake places are different from what they were previously. Even more characteristic of an earthquake is that it signifies changes that are arising from within the earth itself and not coming from outside. The first half of the first sentence quoted above is simply telling us that after the changes have started to manifest on the physical level, the earth will never again be as she is now.

But this does not mean that we will witness a series of gradual mutations. The second half of the sentence makes it clear that we have to be prepared for the total overthrow of the earth holon. If the moon, which we know as a pale light, becomes red, and the sun, which is now red at its rising and setting and bright yellow at noon, becomes dark like a coarse cloth, then the text is speaking of a total switch in the roles that we attribute to different aspects of the earth cosmos. According to the Sixth Seal, it is but a cowardly illusion to hope that the present earth changes will remain on the invisible levels and so pass us by.

In the text accompanying the Sixth Seal, there are further signs pointing towards an extremely far-reaching reordering of the physical earth. If the stars, which we have always seen shining high above us in the firmament, come falling to earth like figs from a tree, we are faced with another symbol which tells us that the newly emerging earth's body might be just the opposite of what we know as today's physical earth. That the falling figs are described as unripe means that we should not expect the changes to follow a logical pattern, at least not in any usual sense. The changes may come breaking in upon us very unexpectedly and in ways beyond our imagination.

The third sentence of the message gives us an idea of the course which the process of the earth changes may take on the physical level. It introduces the image of a scroll being rolled up, signifying that the change will essentially alter the constitution of the earth's ambience. Instead of the uniform configuration which the physical world presents to us today, we will witness a rounded, multi-layered, spherical one. The last part of the sentence emphasizes that the physical features of the geographical earth will have to obey the laws of the earth's new constitution: "...and every mountain and island was jolted out of its place."

Such an overturning of the earth's physical ambience may be a new and doubtless frightening experience for human beings, but certainly not for the planet itself. The geological history of the earth bears testimony to many such upheavals, during which continents disappeared and others emerged. For billions of years, oceans covered lands that today enjoy the sunlight. The age of the human race is obviously too short to have had experience of such a grand restructuring of the planet. Hopefully, we are now sufficiently grown-up to accept it and not be afraid of its cataclysmic aspects.

If you were to ask me when the sixth phase will start, I would suggest that it is already under way. It may only be humanity's persistent denial that significant earth changes are happening that is causing us to designate all the local catastrophes that we watch daily on TV as being casual effects of modern ecological imbalances. In fact, they are exploding with unusual intensity all over the planet.

I have the sense that the restructuring of the earth's physical body will be accomplished through a very great number of small catastrophes, such as we are already witnessing. In this way the crust of the old earth will gradually become sufficiently 'open' to make space for the new body to emerge. But it is only by inter-acting with the other five strands of the earth changing process that these preparatory steps can gather the momentum needed for the radical rebirth of the planet's material body, as suggested by the Sixth Seal.

In mentioning earth's material body, we are touching again on the theme of its geomantic constitution. You will remember that in the Second Chapter we started to explore the powers of the earth and its consciousness. In our discussion of the third of the Seven Apocalyptic Seals we proceeded to the study of the etheric basis of the earth's ambience. This could also be called 'the light-body of the earth'. By diving into the secrets of the Sixth Seal, we can now complete our review of earth's different dimen-sions by getting to know its physical body.

As a culture we consider the material level to be perfectly well known to us, and it may seem ridiculous to make it part of a geomantic exploration.. Surely, we may say, there is nothing more to be explored, apart from a few details. Yet we know it so well only from one point of view. We see the physical reality as stand-ing on its own, separate from the other dimensions which I have mentioned above. Extracted from the totality of the earth cosmos, the physical world seems perfect in itself, and as if no other dimension is needed to complement its life-bearing function.

But the truth is that we can only believe in this restricted view of the earth's ambience because the spiritual constitution of the universe is so perfect that each fractal of its wholeness is per-fect too. This is why the physical dimension of earth's ambience is rounded off and complete in itself, and why we can think of it as the only aspect of reality which exists. Within its material micro-cosm it seems to lack nothing which might be needed for life to appear in all its effectiveness and beauty.

While I was pondering over the story of the Sixth Seal, I asked Julius, my counselor from the nature kingdom, how to more effectively deal with the conflict between humanity's fixed image of the physical world and the unavoidable need for change. While framing my question, I happened to glance at the beautiful sunrise which was especially bright that morning. His answer was as clear as the colors of the sunrise: "It is not possible to ride two horses at the same time. You will have to renounce the beauty of the existing (material) world." And after a while he added: "The earth is caught in the beauty and perfection of its physical appearance. As such it is wonderful but too weak. People have learned to manipulate the material level of existence as they want. There is nothing more for you to learn from the earth as it is now. Put aside any false hopes. It is a fact that the earth will undergo a basic re-ordering of itself, and this means that you too will have to make drastic changes in your attitude toward the planet."

I felt he was referring to the dream from which I had just awakened. I had dreamed that night that I had been visited by a woman whose task it was to revise my work. She went carefully through my files, but found no mistakes other an error I had made while buying a washing machine. I was upset, asserting that the purchase of a washing machine had nothing to do with the spiritual nature of my work. Yet she insisted that truth should prevail in each and every detail. I got mad. To mock her, I began attaching tiny pictures of different types of washing machines to my chest, shouting at her the while, "Is this my identity? Is this my identity?" But to my surprise, whenever I put a picture of a washing machine in front of my heart, it turned instantly into a cosmogram...

Obviously, my mistake had been to exaggerate the meaning of the invisible levels of reality and neglect the role of the physical world both in daily life and in the process of the earth changes. Subconsciously, I may already have thought of it as lost to the future, because I was identifying it with the mechanistic way in which our civilization treats the material level.

The instant transformation of washing machines into cosmograms suggests that matter possesses an unknown but highly interesting quality, which might be demonstrated if the prevailing rationalistic view of what constitutes reality did not push it into the passive role of 'hardware'. The physical dimension of existence could reveal itself in its role as a means of communication between the different dimensions of the cosmos. In fact, the era of cybernetics is already introducing the transmutation that is leading us towards the 'soft' function of matter. All the different dimensions of the cosmos could meet on the level of the incarnated life-body, and so become condensed in a unity that would make life strong and beautiful beyond all imagination.

But to be able to serve as the communicator between the different dimensions of the universe, the quality of the material earth must be made more transparent and flexible. The message accompanying the Sixth Seal reassures us that the planet is heading in this direction through the cycles of the earth changes, and that the necessary physical-level changes are in preparation.

Finally, readers would expect that, through the Seventh and last of the Apocalyptic Seals, they will get to know the final and most decisive phase of the tormented earth's rebirth. Nothing so simple! We are told, "Then, when he had broken the seventh seal, there was utter silence in Heaven for what seemed to me half-an-hour." (Rev 8:1) After this break, which breathes expectancy, the Seven Angels sounded their trumpets to prepare the scene for the Last Judgment, which is a layer of the Apocalypse discussed in Chapter 4. Only afterwards does the text return to the Seven Seals, to continue the revelatory story about the phases of the process of the earth changes.

After the Seven Angels had sounded their trumpets, the Seven Thunders lifted up their voices and Saint John wanted to write their message down, as he had done for the previous six seals. But he was stopped by a voice from heaven which forbade him to do so. Instead, he was urged to take and eat a little book (containing the secret of the Seventh Seal) from the hands of the angel standing in front of him: "'Take it,' he said to him, 'and eat it up. It will be bitter to your stomach, but sweet as honey in your mouth.' Then he took the little book from the angel's hand and swallowed it. It was as sweet as honey to the taste but when he had eaten it up it was bitter to his stomach." (Rev 10:9)

This passage is telling us in symbolic language that it is not possible for the human mind to comprehend the nature of the changes that will finally push the 'new earth' into existence. This is why it was useless to write down the message of the Seventh

Seal. The only way it can be known is through feeling and intuition. These can be equated with one's innermost experience, symbolized in Revelation by 'eating the message and tasting it in one's mouth and stomach'.

Even if we cannot understand the last stage of the earth changes, the Book of Revelation still lets us know, covertly, the final outcome of the phase of the Seventh Seal. It is presented in the last part of the Apocalypse by way of the seven basic qualities attributed to the New Jerusalem. As I have already mentioned, the New Jerusalem is to be seen as the symbol of the new earth cosmos after the successful completion of the changes.

Let me list those seven qualities of the renewed earth cosmos, in accordance with their description in the 21st and 22nd Chapter of the Revelation of St. John.

1. While undergoing the torments of transmutation revealed in the Sixth Seal, the physical matter of the old earth is etherified. It is distilled to attain the translucence that we know in precious stones and crystals. One could equate the matter of the future earth with the quality of etheric matter, to describe which Revelation reaches for the help of brilliant stones and shining gold: "Her brilliance sparkled like a very precious jewel with the clear light of crystal...The wall itself was built of translucent stone, while the city was of purest gold, with the brilliance of glass." (Rev 21:11 and 18)

2. There is no need for religious institutions whose role is to mediate between human beings and their divine origin. People will come to know the immediate presence of Divinity within their own personal holon. Told in the language of Revelation 21 and 22, "I could see no Sanctuary in the city, for the Lord, the Almighty God, and the Lamb are themselves its Sanctuary."

3. The new constitution of the earth cosmos will be fed by light and power from within. Instead of being lit from outside as at the present day, the new earth will shine from within its center, as do the stars. The symbolism of Revelation indicates that the light shining from within the heart of the planet will have, not a physical, but a spiritual and emotional quality: "The city has no need for the light of sun or moon, for the splendor of God fills it with light and its radiance is the Lamb." (Rev 21:23)

Seals	Symbol	Quality	Earth Change Phenomena
First Seal	Rider on a white horse	Element Air	New quality of earth radiation—light-islands appear
Second Seal	Rider on a red horse	Element Fire	Archetypal powers of the earth activated—transformation of elemental beings
Third Seal	Rider on a black horse	Element Earth	The changing light body of the earth
Fourth Seal	Rider on a horse sickly green in color	Element Water	The voices of ancestors are to be heard—the powers of darkness are to be integrated
Fifth Seal	Souls in white garments	Human	Process of human transformation
Sixth Seal	Earthquake	Space/time	Planetary transformation
Seventh Seal	Seven thunders	Earth cosmos	Seven qualities of the new earth cosmos

The seven seals as related to the phases of the earth changes

4. The new constitution of the earth cosmos does not know the duality of good and evil or of light and dark. The shadow aspects are to be integrated into the dynamics of the whole and will complement the light aspects. To express this, a rather heretical thought for Christian doctrine, Revelation uses the symbol of the city's gates, which in ancient times used to be shut at night and opened again at dawn. "The city's gates shall stand open day after day — and there will be no night there." (Rev 21:25)

5. "Then he showed me the river of the Water of Life, sparkling like crystal as it flowed from the throne of God and of the Lamb." (Rev 22:1) The River of Life flowing through the center of the earth cosmos signifies the power of the reunited life forces. During the present, but now passing, phase of earth's evolution, the different dimensions of life have been torn apart so that they appear on either the visible or invisible planes of reality. The multidimensional constitution of the new earth makes possible the simultaneous appearance of all of life's different dimensions. As a result the life force will become powerful and potent beyond all imagination.

6. Everyday life will have the qualities of temporality and eternity fused in one whole. This means that the boundaries dividing heaven from earth will cease to exist. This is an illogical situation that cannot be comprehended by the linear mind. As already mentioned, the Bible expresses the astonishing synthesis of mortal life and eternity in the symbolic image of the Tree of Eternal Life: "...on either bank of the river grew the Tree of Life." (Rev 22:2) It is beyond all logic that a tree should grow on both sides of a river simultaneously!

7. The verse continues, "The leaves of the Tree were for healing of the nations." Participation in the holistic life processes of the new earth cosmos will make it possible for different races and nations to cooperate creatively with each other, beyond any thought of competition. This in turn will enable the healing of the old wounds and conflicts derived from our past history.

Chapter Seven

The Balkan Experience — Reappearance of Evil?

A feeling of disappointment prevailed when the recent wars started on the Balkan peninsula, beginning in my home country of Slovenia. We were lucky that the war in Slovenia lasted only for a week after we had declared sovereignty. It has been much more difficult for other Balkan nations like the Bosnians, Croats, Serbs and Albanians, who for seven years were caught in the most violent and humiliating mutual fighting, warfare and ethnic cleansing. Even today the conflicts are not solved.

We are members of the advanced Western culture and for years now we have been ashamed to watch television and see the thousands of despairing refugees and the blood-soaked victims, and hear the voices of the countless numbers of women who had been raped. We had felt sure that after the disaster of the Second World War we had changed, never to slide back into such an upheaval again. And yet, at the close of the 20th century, the retrogression is so obvious that even the successful peace treaties cannot hide it.

There are of course political, social and economic causes for the apocalyptic Balkan wars during the nineties. But I believe we all share feelings and intuitions about the upheavals, and if we pay any regard to them, we may agree that there must be other causes, such as ones of a psychic nature.

If the constitution of the European continent were compared to that of the human body, the Balkans would represent its belly. In terms of the psyche of our modern culture, this means that the Balkans stand for the European subconscious, the area where there lie suppressed the problems which our Western culture was never able to solve. For example, the historic split within the Christian Church resulted in a border separating the Orthodox and Catholic Churches which still runs right across Bosnia today. Another of the general problems related to European culture is the confrontation with Islam. It found an echo in the wars between the Austrian and Turkish empires that for centuries were fought on Balkan soil.

No less traumatic was the suppression in the 15th century of the medieval movement of the Bogumils. This was carried out by a crusade dispatched under the authority of the Roman Catholic Church. As I mentioned in Chapter 5, the Bogumils, like the Cathars in France, had turned away from the official Church because they believed that the Christ was not to be sought in rituals and other expressions of devotion, but within the divine spark that represents the center of one's own being. The Bosnian kingdom supported the Bogumils, but the severity of the crusade's assault made it easy for the Turks to conquer it. Disillusioned with Christianity, the whole Bosnian nation converted to Islam. This is why, in the midst of the Christian Balkans, there is a Slavic nation which holds firmly to Islam, creating a situation which is hard to handle.

Yet similar religious and socio-economic problems could be alleged as being responsible for the expansion of evil in Ireland, and in the Caucasus also, where blood is being shed now, at the end of the 20th century. This would suggest that there was still another reason for the impact that the disastrous chain of events connected with the Balkans had on our global awareness.

The first intuition of its real significance was conveyed to my consciousness through a dream focused on a place in Bosnia, in the center of the Balkans. The name of the place is Velika Kladusa. On January 14th, 1999, I dreamed that I was traveling with my wife Marika on an Intercity Express train across the territory of the former Yugoslavia. It was the most modern and fastest kind of train, developed by German Rail. Completely white in color and fashionably designed, it represents the highest level that modern train technology has yet reached.

According to the timetable, there was to be a half-hour stop in Velika Kladusa so that travelers could walk about and stretch their legs after the long session sitting in the train. Marika and I also took a walk through the small town. I was amazed at the primitive simplicity of the place, which some stupid intrusions of modern housing made seem chaotic. Some of the small, dark-colored cottages were even roofed with thatch. There was a screaming contrast between the ancient feel of the small town and the super-technology of our Intercity Express train.

When we returned to the train and were waiting to continue our journey, my wife started to criticize humanitarian organizations. She had seen reports that one of them was engaged in financial anomalies and misuse of funds. Her theme was that officially they are working for the highest good, yet secretly striving for profit. I got angry with Marika and accused her of condemning the very people who are working for the good and the just. Upset by her criticism, I made a big show of standing up and leaving the train in a rage.

Very soon, feeling sorry for my overreaction, I turned round and ran back to the railway station. But it was too late. The white train had gone and Marika with it. Quickly I started to search up and down the railway station, holding onto the hope that I might find it on some other track. It had obviously gone. What I did see were some old, pale-green colored train wagons, slightly decayed and obviously no longer in use. They were in the glass-covered station hall which, to my surprise, had three stories, all of them filled with the stationary wagons. There was no locomotive to be seen, also no trace of my super-modern train. Gazing at this timeless machinery still standing before me, I felt lost...

When I awoke and in my meditation attuned to the quality of the Intercity Express, I felt an extremely quick and nervous vibration high in the top of my head. Tuning into the three-story station with the ancient wagons, my attention was pulled down into the depths of my belly. There, the dynamics slowed right down, almost to point zero.

The fast-moving linear composition of the Express train is easily understood as symbolizing our high-tech Western civilization. It also stands for a particular constitution of time that we know as linear. This runs in a mechanical rhythm, from minute to minute and from century to century. The ancient, unmoving and obscure culture of Velika Kladusa is its opposite. Instead of being linearly composed, the trains were standing one above the other on three floors, to form a kind of a rounded circular space characteristic of the cyclical model of time.

The juxtaposition of the high-tech train with the straw-thatched huts of Velika Kladusa conveyed a definite message: that aspect of the human being which belongs to the evolution of nature cannot successfully keep pace with the speedy development of our culture. To put it in another way, the mental and linear thrust involved in our forms of civilization tends to submerge the space of the psyche which is emotionally rounded. If our evolution continues to follow such a trend, there is a real danger that human beings will get torn apart. Our head, lifted high in the perfection of mental activity, will no longer be able to understand and accept the 'dirty' womb of emotions below.

In consequence, a most dangerous abyss is emerging between the positive and uplifting development of civilization on the one hand, and the violent, rapacious and bloodthirsty reality of human life on the other. It is a general problem, of which the Balkan events are representative. In the planetary economy it corresponds to the explosive opposites embodied by the rich 'West' and the poor 'Third World'. An even more dangerous manifestation of this gaping abyss is the ever-growing misuse of drugs. Individuals who are violated by the mental domination of our rational civilization turn to them as the most obvious substitute for the psychic wholeness for which they yearn.

The violence of one's culture affects one's own emotional integrity and creates a confusing emotional upheaval 'down there in the intestines'. Failure to understand its cause could drive the world-mind mad. It could start to throw bombs and rockets at the emotional hell, without realizing that one part of the human being was attacking its own complement, and that both mind and emotions represent equally important parts of one and the same organism. When the Western alliance started to bomb Serbia in April 1999, I had a strong feeling that this tragic situation was manifesting in harsh reality.

If we are to prevent this kind of possible 'third world war catastrophe', we need to become aware that the abyss is primarily within ourselves, that is, within those of us who have taken the path of civilization guided by the mind. Confrontations like those surfacing in the Balkans are only an effect of the split within each one of us, as individual human beings. Only by working to connect the sexual, emotional and heart-feeling qualities of our being with the mental and rational ones can we prevent civilization from ultimately breaking apart into opposite poles which would most tragically destroy each other.

The path that one needs to take is a most sensitive one. It is not enough, for example, to store information in one's mind about different teachings on how to get in touch with the subtle realities of nature and its emotional or etheric worlds. One needs to embody them and exercise them practically, so that the emotional level of human psyche can also get used to the different type of reality. On the other hand, initiation into some shamanistic rituals or spiritual patterns is insufficient if they are not integrated into one's mental concepts and modes of behavior, so that they influence one's daily activity.

To build a new culture of peace, we need first of all to cross-connect those parts within ourselves that are at present potentially at odds. The complex composed of mind, reason and knowledge has to be infused with the emotional, sexual and soul qualities which are equally important 'ingredients' of our being.

The message of the dream of the Express train focuses on one of the main obstacles that prevent this merging of the polarities within our being. It was symbolized by my getting upset with Marika's sharp criticism of organizations which are working for the good and positive in the world. At first I was deeply offended by her outlandish point of view. How can someone be selflessly working for the light and the good, but, as she supposed, have financial appetites hidden in the background, i.e. be working for the bad?

Yet, when I started running away from her, it was only a moment before I turned round to get back to my train, because I glimpsed that in a strange way Marika was right. Her distrust of humanitarian organizations that commit financial abuse has to be understood symbolically. It is in effect a severe criticism of the one-sided striving towards the good and the light and the positive that is the basis of our culture. The problem is that we invest our powers as individuals and as a civilization in only one aspect of totality — the one that according to our preconceptions is considered worthy and positive — and when we do so, we push several extensions of life's totality into the roles of darkness, evil and negativity. As a result, striving for the light can become the worst embodiment of evil.

In my dream, the primary reason for my upset was the dangerous contradiction inherent in willing only the good and the positive. It is not possible to understand the logic of this as long as one's mind is looking at it from the outside. Only after my anger had got my emotions established in my body could I accept the provocative idea that the dark forces are being fed by our own one-sided patterns of thought and action dedicated exclusively to 'the highest good'.

At one point in our conversation, my master from the elemental world, Julius, commented that our culture is drowning in the will for the good and positive. We are ready to commit the worst in order to further what we consider to be positive. At its midpoint, the Revelation of St. John suggests how we may reconcile this basic contradiction within the human being and our human culture. I am referring to Chapters 11 and 13, which — together with Chapter 12 — represent the central portion of the text in its totality of 22 chapters. Chapter 11 tells the story of the Two (divine) Witnesses, Chapter 13 the story of the Two Beasts[1].

The Two Witnesses represent the wholeness of the human soul. By soul I mean that aspect of the human being that belongs to eternity even when incarnated on earth and therefore subject to the conditions of time. The Two Witnesses are presented as walking on the earth and meeting the challenges of everyday life, but also as having supernatural powers. They are reported to have the power, "to shut up the sky and stop any rain from falling during the time of their preaching." (Rev 11:6) Their power is obviously identical with the spiritual powers of nature and the cosmos in general. They can be recognized as the ancestors who

---

1 The translation of the New Testament in modern English by J.B.Phillips calls the Two Beasts, 'Two Animals'. So as not to cast aspersions upon the animal kingdom, I use the word, 'Beasts', as do some other translations.

live beyond the limitations of the physical world, and have at their disposal the full powers of the soul.

Yet at the same time they are involved in the tumults of the material world, and this makes me believe that they also simultaneously represent the spiritual powers of the incarnated human soul. The story of the Two Witnesses depicts in a very tangible way the destiny of the human soul as it faces the challenge of material incarnation: they will be conquered and killed and "their bodies will lie in the street of the great city... the very place where their Lord himself was crucified. For three and a half days men from all peoples and tribes and languages and nations will gaze upon their bodies and will not allow them to be buried." (Rev 11:8)

"But after three and a half days the Spirit of life from God entered them and they stood upright on their feet. This struck terror into the hearts of those who were watching them, and they heard a tremendous voice speaking to these two from Heaven, saying, 'Come up here!' And they went up to Heaven in a cloud in full view of their enemies." (Rev 11:11)

Even though the laws of material life distract the human personality from the context of its holistic soul, when it is lifted out of the body after physical death it can re-unite with eternity. The cycle of birth and death ensures that the physical experience of the incarnated life can be accomplished, and yet the fundamental oneness with the soul's integrity cannot be lost. It only becomes dangerous if people start to obey those forces within their mental or emotional world that do not know the fundamental unity of the cosmos. These forces are an expression of the separated poles within the human being and were depicted in my dream by the white line of the Intercity Express on the one hand, and on the other by the dark habitations of Velika Kladusa in the Balkans.

The Revelation of St. John presents the two sundered polarities as objectified powers that are influencing our civilization quite fatally. They are symbolized by the Two Beasts. After the Evil had been thrown down to earth, as described in the 12th Chapter, the 13th Chapter tells of one of the Beasts appearing out of the Water and the other out of the Earth.

"Then, as I stood on the sand of the sea-shore, there rose out of the sea before my eyes an animal with seven heads and ten horns. There were diadems upon its horns and blasphemous names upon its heads." (Rev 13:1) "So it poured out blasphemies against God, blaspheming his name and his dwelling-place and those who live in Heaven. Moreover, it was permitted to make war upon the saints and to conquer them; the authority given to it extended over every tribe and people and language and nation. All the inhabitants of earth will worship it..." (Rev 13:6) The Element of Water is a synonym for the emotional quality. The beast appearing out of the Water therefore stands for the emotions, but its behavior shows that it lacks their integrative power. It is hostile towards anything that has the power to connect the separate aspects of life and round them off into a greater whole. In the testimony of St. John, this greater whole is depicted as the power of the divine word and the power of saints, i.e., of those who are in tune with the vibration of the Word.

The second Beast — rising out of the Earth — represents the hardened power of human rationality which has lost its basic understanding of the spiritual nature of life and matter. It is going to use the magical properties of the material world to build a civilization that is split off from the totality of life. "Then I saw another animal rising out of the earth, and it had two horns like a lamb but it spoke in the voice of a dragon." (Rev 13:11) The powers of the second beast work to seduce the human masses into enjoying the illusion of the separated world condition, and even into making them believe that they are taking part in the reality of life itself. This is the reason why the beast appears out of the earth as a lamb and yet talks with the voice of a dragon. It is a destructive power that wears the mask of a humble servant who caters to the needs of humanity.

The following descriptions resemble my description of the Intercity Express. The technological 'miracles' of 20th century civilization are made to appear before our eyes in the language of two millennia past: "It performs great signs: before men's eyes it makes fire fall down from heaven to earth." And: "It was allowed to give the breath of life to the statue of the animal so that the statue could speak and condemn to death all those who do not worship its statue." There are also allusions to the use of credit and identity cards, which penetrate all levels of our everyday life: "Then it compels all, small and great, rich and poor, free men and slaves, to receive a mark on their right hands or on their foreheads. The purpose of this is that no one should be able to buy or sell unless he bears the mark of the name of the animal or the number of its name." (Rev 13:13-17)

The Revelation of St. John does not only make clear the destructive nature of both the forces personifying human fragmentation, it also makes clear the divine origin of both 'Beasts'. In Chapter 12 it reveals their cosmic background. I refer to the battle between the mighty Angel Michael and the equally powerful dragon who bears the name of Satan. The text witnesses that Satan represents an aspect of the angelic world: "Then war broke out in Heaven. Michael and his angels battled with the dragon. The dragon and his angels fought back, but they did not prevail and they were expelled from Heaven. So the huge dragon, the serpent of the ancient times, who is called the devil and Satan, the deceiver of the whole world, was hurled down upon the earth, and his angels were hurled down with him." (Rev 12:7)

The fighting in Heaven is a symbol testifying that both parties, the victorious Michael with his angels and Satan "hurled down upon the earth with his angels," represent two different aspects of the angelic world. The angelic world moreover is a symbol of what could be called the universal consciousness. Michael stands for the light and the "serpent of the ancient times" for the dark aspect of the cosmic consciousness.

Michael with his light-sword represents the divine powers that inspire the universe to expand and grow in beauty and life-giving power. The "serpent of the ancient times" represents those forces of the divine that are opposed to the expansion, and so prevent the universe from spilling over across its boundaries and toppling into self-destruction. Opposing the new, they hold to "the ancient." Here is the lesson that modern ecology has taught us once again: unlimited expansion means self-destruction.

The healthy development of life is made secure only if both forces, those which drive forward and those which hold back, are kept in proper proportion one to the other. The impulse to grow should be equaled by a corresponding injection of the power which holds back to point zero, to the dark infinity of Nothing.

Of course, the universe would cease to expand and stagnation set in if the inhibiting function of the forces of darkness were to become too strong. To ensure that the creation of the cosmos will continue, the powers of light, embodied within Christian thought by the Archangel Michael, have to 'fight' their way through and secure their preponderance.

In painting an image of the war in heaven, Revelation is very precise in its presentation of the role of Michael and the powers aligned with him. They are winning, but that does not mean that they are better than the opposing powers which are being defeated. Michael is winning, not to destroy the "serpent of the ancient times" but to mark out the proper proportion between the forces of light and the equally divine forces of darkness. It is the role of Michael, and of the aspect of the angelic world that he represents, to protect the new ways that are the chosen path of the universal evolution. By inspiring all the different subjects and co-creators of cosmic evolution to take those paths and manifest them in the life of planets and galaxies, he makes sure that the forces of darkness do not take over and force the divine creative word to be mute[2].

Within the framework of theological thought, this is a very delicate point. Usually the 'battle in heaven' has been taken literally as a call to follow Michael and fight against darkness and evil — and also against things feminine. You must use all possible means to win, for otherwise you are betraying the divine will!

This is a very dangerous dualistic thought pattern that creates enemies, empowers strong and ruthless people and demands well equipped armies, so that it can say, "The darkness has to be defeated if we are to enjoy freedom, democracy and human rights. Fight for the good and the light!" It is a thought pattern that stands directly opposed to the culture of peace for which we are striving.

Seen in the mirror of the Revelation of St. John, this same thought pattern causes us to distrust the cosmic context of the earth's evolution and denigrate the earth as an unhealthy place in

2 On the role of Michael, see my book *Christ Power and the Earth Goddess*, pages 26-27.

the universe, one where the devil has been relegated. Misrepresenting the earth as the place assigned to Satan to be his last dwelling-place, it ignites hatred towards the Mother Earth and the powers of life that she selflessly offers to us all.

We need mental and emotional clarity and discipline to recognize all the diverse and continuing manifestations of this false thought pattern: it emerges in the way we think of political trends, the way we talk and feel about our neighbors, and finally in the way we see God and comprehend the nature of life itself. One should make sure that one is not a divider, rather one must seek the path of integration. The imperative of the future is to find creative ways to integrate opposites, and not get entangled in their wars.

My thought goes back to the theme of the Fourth Apocalyptic Seal, with "death riding on a horse sickly green in color." It says there that one quarter of the world submits to its power. In Chapter 4 we have equated this quarter with the backspace of our body, which has long since been lost to our awareness. In referring to the universal dimensions, the famous abbess, writer and healer from the Middle Ages, Hildegard von Bingen (1098-1179), assigns this "backspace" to the "Angels of Darkness". Her insights are extremely clear[3].

She argues that if the Divinity is to be understood as totality from which nothing can be excluded, then darkness, shadow and evil are also part of its wholeness. But, she says, only those of the highest angelic rank, the ones called the Cherubim, are strong enough to carry the light as well as the dark in their consciousness. If the Cherubim of Light are taking over three quarters of the heavens, the fourth one belongs to the Cherubim of Darkness, to be their divine domain.

The "war in Heaven" reported in the 12th Chapter of Revelation informs us that at one point in the evolution of the cosmos the focus of the Cherubim of Darkness was transferred to the earth. I believe that that point in time to be identical with the

---

3 See the chapter on Hildegard von Bingen in *The Physics of Angels. A Realm where Spirit and Science Meet*, Matthew Fox & Rupert Sheldrake, Harper San Francisco 1996.

moment when human beings were 'expelled from paradise'. At the same time that people got the right to use the dangerous power of their free will, the universal consciousness had to take precautions to ensure that the possible emergence of human destructiveness would not spill over and infect the whole universe. As a result the forces of darkness merged their force-fields with the earth's. In the words of Revelation, Satan and his angels — the Cherubim of Darkness — were "hurled down upon the earth."

As a result, development on the earth plane took on forms unknown in the earlier phase of the planet's evolution, the one that is usually equated with the image of Paradise. From that time forward, whenever people tried to push their egotistic, ignorant, deceptive, etc., powers onto life's web, the (divine) forces of evil would be provoked to hit back in the same way but with redoubled force. These are not acts done out of hatred — even if they often seem such — but are an appropriate way to teach human beings who can – because of their free will — ignore any other kind of lesson. Too often, we are only ready to listen when the pain reaches way down into our belly, so that the very foundation of the emotional psyche is shattered.

Satan, the "serpent of the ancient times," became the all-powerful inquisitor of human actions, putting to the proof everything created by the human mind or emotions. His divinely appointed task is to make it obvious whether human deeds belong to the wholeness and holiness of the universe, or are a mere result of the egocentric will.

The 'Lord of Darkness' has gradually 'incarnated' within both polarities, the emotional and rational halves of the separated human world. The two 'incarnations' of the cosmic evil are depicted in the Revelation of St. John as the 'beast emerging from the water' and the one 'emerging from the earth'. They jointly mirror the misery of the human race when trapped in separation and illusion[4].

---

4 The Austrian philosopher and spiritual teacher Rudolf Steiner speaks of the Two Beasts as representative of Lucifer and Ahriman, Lucifer pushing one-sidedly towards light and Ahriman towards the darkness of matter. Steiner's works refer to them as the two temptations facing the human race. The Christ path leads between them.

My profession is earth healing, and all too often in the course of my work I have had the opportunity of experiencing what we are accustomed to call 'the dark power'. It has its fingers in all the places of the earth on which people have projected their egocentric ideas and preconceptions and used them according to their selfish needs. Working with places like this to heal, revitalize and re-balance their energy fields means also to confront their inherent shadows and free the place from their rule.

This has given me countless opportunities to encounter and be challenged by the forces of the dark[5]. Too often I have had to endure the power of their counter-stroke after successfully initiating healing work on a place which had been destroyed. Since we also work in this field as a family, our home has time and again been put under immense pressure or even broken into and devastated energetically. At times I have almost been in despair because the dominance of 'the dark power' seemed never ending.

To my surprise the situation changed radically during the second half of August 1997. I noticed the change after we had returned from Tibet with my daughter Ana and the Idriart Festival group. The group of 24 dedicated people had done the basic healing work on the etheric organs of Tibet's capital Lhasa, guided by the Angel of Earth Healing channeled by Ana. We were free to do this as part of the Idriart festival art programs there[6].

After returning home and continuing with my work in Europe, I soon noticed that the shadow powers had ceased their usual vigorous opposition. At first I didn't dare to talk about the astonishing change publicly. But now, almost three years later, I can give testimony that I have never again experienced the aggressive presence of 'the dark powers' as I did before.

I believe that there must have been a decree at the level of the cosmic consciousness, issued in late August 1997, to pull the powers of the 'cherubim of darkness' out of the force-field of the earth. This was done to enable the earth changing process to

---

5 Instances of meeting with powers of darkness are reported in the chapter on 'Dealing with Destructive Forces' in my book *Healing the Heart of the Earth*.
6 My brother Miha Pogačnik founded The International Foundation IDRIART to build bridges between cultures and nations through art.

start. In effect, it was only a month later that I noticed the first surprising variations in the patterns of the ground radiation of the earth. Eventually these led to the radical change in the aura of the earth which was completed between February and April 1998 and about which I reported in the first chapter of this book.

In fact, the Revelation of St. John also speaks of the withdrawal of the dark force from the earth during the course of the predicted earth changes. Chapter 20 tells us that only after 'Satan has been bound for a thousand years', can the New Jerusalem be revealed: "Then I saw an angel coming down from Heaven with the key of the pit and a huge chain in his hand. He seized the dragon, the serpent of the ancient days, who is both the devil and Satan, and bound him fast for a thousand years. Then he hurled him into the pit, and locked and sealed it over his head, so that he could deceive the nations no more until the thousand years were past. But then he must be set free for a little while." (Rev 20:1)

The above verses make clear first of all that the withdrawal of the forces of darkness from the power-fields of the earth was due to a decision within the cosmic consciousness. This is symbolized by an 'angel coming down from Heaven'. Secondly it states that the retreat of Satan can only be of a temporary nature: "Then, when the thousand years are over, Satan will be released from his prison, and will set out to deceive the nations in the four corners of the earth, Gog and Magog, and to lead them into battle. They will be as numerous as the sand of the seashore." (Rev 20:7)

The withdrawal of the dark forces can only be temporary because, first, they belong to the cosmic order and cannot be finally destroyed. Their rhythmic appearance and disappearance is governed by the need for their powers to balance the powers of light in the process of the universal evolution, and this dictates the situation and manner of their introduction and withdrawal. Secondly, the forces of darkness cannot simply disappear from human history as long as human beings retain the full freedom to use their will as they choose. Free will makes it possible for any human being to pull in the powers of the shadow, whenever that person decides. This may be done consciously by following the plan of some person or group to use the divine power of life to hurt, torture, or even kill. It can also happen subconsciously by someone cradling bad feelings and destructive thoughts about another, or simply by closing one's heart to truth.

This is why not much has changed in human affairs since 1997 and the presumed withdrawal of the 'Cherubim of Darkness' from the earth. The situation has the character of a tragedy. After millennia of pressure and terror, people could finally take a deep breath and relax. As a gift from the spiritual world, the cause of all evil was gone from the earth. But instead of realizing how lucky we are, many of our co-citizens are continuing to follow the patterns of behavior built up during the reign of the 'Two Beasts'. In so doing, their personal emotions, thoughts and actions are forcing the return of the powers which had retired.

The only way to avoid contributing to the conceivable reappearance of evil at the threshold of the 21st century is to attune personally, again and again, to the true nature of life in the here and now, and not get automatically stuck in the past. The past has gone already. Be what you are now. This decision must be supported by consciously renouncing the repetition of past emotional and ideological patterns. This must be done again and again.

Remember that the future demands a rounding off and integration on all levels of existence. In effect, there can be no final withdrawal of the destructive forces from our history, or from our personal life, as long as we do not learn how to integrate them into our lives as a co-creative force.

In my experience the integrative process starts by making a personal effort to detect a positive aspect in any situation, no matter how tragic or destructive. If you are not already practicing this kind of discipline, try it now. Of course, this does not mean that one has to accept something that does not feel right ethically or morally. One should follow the teaching of the Seventh Letter addressed to the Angel of Laodicea and in any situation make a clear decision. But while your heart or your mind is urging you to say 'no', always look as well for the aspect to which you can wholeheartedly say 'yes'.

In this way we shall avoid binding the dark powers forcefully back to the earth after the planet has been decreed free of their influence. Even more importantly, by learning how to weave the dark side of reality into the life process in such a way that it complements its light-giving counterpart, our life will find a new creative impetus and strength beyond our present comprehension. As long as opposites, such as light and dark, positive and negative, left and right..., are separated in our consciousness and within our emotional and etheric force-fields, we will tend to be weak and vulnerable. To put it symbolically, we operate at not much more than 6% of our strength and creative power. In this state of being we are effectively asleep, compared to what we really are. If the integrative process connecting the dark and the light within us comes into play, the polarities start to reinforce each other and an unprecedented awakening gets underway.

Do you remember the story of the Sleeping Beauty from your childhood[7]? Read it again! It testifies that it is the exclusion of the dark powers from the totality of our life that thrusts the manifold potentials of the human being into a state of deep sleep. As you may remember, the plot of the story that led the Sleeping Beauty to fall asleep for 'a hundred years' originates with the decision of her father, the king, to invite only the twelve fairies of light to the celebration of his daughter's birth. He consciously excluded the thirteenth one, who is a black fairy, arguing that he had only twelve golden plates and spoons at his disposal.

Disregarding the plans for the ceremony, the black fairy appeared and predicted the princess' death. The unexpected appearance of the black fairy corresponds to the apocalyptic story of Satan, "the serpent of the ancient times" who was hurled down upon the earth. The Revelation of St. John comments on the descent of the 'black fairy' to the earth in this way: "Therefore, rejoice, O Heavens, and all you who live in the Heavens! But alas for the earth and the sea, for the devil has come down to you in great fury, knowing that his time is short." (Rev 12:12) The time is short because, according to the information stored within the tale of the Sleeping Beauty, it is limited to the symbolic hundred years.

Can you imagine what an awful situation it is for the guests

---

7 The two brothers Grimm wrote down the folk tale of the Sleeping Beauty in the central area of Germany in the late 18th century.

invited to the solemn ceremony when the black fairy appears among the 12 fairies of brilliant light. She represents the powers of darkness, which have been provoked at the very moment that human free will has been admitted to the circle of power. All the fairies of light could do to save the new-born baby was to change the threat of death, delivered by their black companion, into the exile of a hundred year's sleep.

No matter how conscientiously her father the king looked after his daughter to make sure she did not hurt herself by touching a spindle — which the black fairy had predicted would doom the princess to a sleep of ages — it still happened. One day, alone in the castle, she was searching through the halls of her consciousness and discovered a small room in a remote tower, which is where the potential of the rational mind abides, spinning at its 'curious wheels'. While she was asking the old crone sitting behind the spinning wheel what the sweet toy of rational thinking was all about, she pricked her finger and immediately fell asleep for 'a hundred years'.

The point that has special meaning for all of us who are interested in the destiny of the earth is that, together with the Sleeping Beauty, her whole environment instantly fell asleep. Told in the words of the fairy tale: "Together with the Sleeping Beauty the whole castle fell asleep ... the horses slept in their stables, and the dogs in the courtyard, the doves on the roof, and the flies on the walls. Even the fire burning on the hearth left off blazing and went to sleep... The wind too died down, and in the trees not one leaf was stirring."

The fairy tale is telling us about a real situation that has deeply affected human destiny. Translated, it says that our discovery of the multiple potentials of free will when connected to rational thought systems, together with the possible misuse of those gifts, has immediately pulled in the presence of the dark forces. Not only did the 'Cherubim of Darkness' penetrate the human power-fields and freeze them to the level of a deep sleep, but simultaneously the force-fields of the earth have been so deeply frozen that matter has hardened to the state that we know today. Hence, no trace of the subtle dimensions could exist on the material level any more. So there came into being the crust of the one-dimensional earth, which we talked about with my friend Julius in Chapter 2.

Told in the words of the fairy tale, "Around the castle a thick layer of brambles started to grow, which from year to year grew thicker and finally overgrew the whole castle, so that no-one could see it, not even the flag on the roof." Only after the passage of the symbolic hundred years and after the 'Cherubim of Darkness' had withdrawn their powers from the earth's force-fields — I have identified the month as August 1997 — could the cycle of the earth changes start, and with it the process of the planet's transmutation. In the imagery of the fairy tale, it is depicted as the sudden transformation of the brambles into flowering roses. The way was open for the prince to awaken the Sleeping Beauty and marry her, inaugurating a new phase of the earth's evolution.

That roses are chosen to be the symbol of the new state of consciousness illustrates the precise symbolism of the tale of the Sleeping Beauty. Roses have not only their beautiful flowers to display, but they also have thorns just as the dull brambles do. Yet in the case of the roses, the dark power of the thorns has been integrated into a balanced whole where the flowers of light play the dominant role, but the powers of the dark also have their function.

Chapter Eight

How the Revelation of St John Mirrors the Changed Earth Cosmos

Up till now we have been moving freely through the Apocalypse as if gliding through a star system. We have paid attention to each of the Seven Seals and to each of the Letters to the Seven Churches in Asia Minor; we have worked on decoding the seven basic qualities of the New Jerusalem and held our breath while confronting the mystery of evil and the Two Beasts. Each of these 'stars' itself conveys an important message. But together, and with many of the other visions and insights written down by the Apostle John, they compose a very complex whole which mirrors the essence of the emerging earth cosmos.

Similarly, we have been considering the earth changes as a succession of separate phenomena, occurring both on the vital-energy level and in the emotional world. We have observed them in the framework of consciousness as well as in their relationship to different facets of life. Now we are ready to look at them from the very broadest prospective, so we can perceive the emerging earth cosmos in all its complexity, and not just scan its separate bits and pieces.

To put it plainly, this means nothing less than asking what will be the role within the renewed earth cosmos of that divine principle that people around the planet are accustomed either to call God, or think of as the spiritual basis upon which the universe dances its eternal dance.

Up till now the visions and insights offered by Revelation have proved a most accurate key for the understanding of the transmutation in which we are involved, both personally and as an evolutionary species. So why should we not use the same key when we dive into the secrets of the spiritual dimensions of the renewed earth cosmos? But first we should pause. To find the answers to our questions, we should enter the text through its proper door, and not just anywhere as we did previously. The problem, as already mentioned, is that Revelation has two doors, one at the very beginning of the book and the other one, marked by the 12th Chapter, at its center. Which should we take first? Let's start at the front door.

The writer of Revelation names himself simply 'John', and I will do the same. The words of Revelation came to John unexpectedly, while he was preaching the gospel of Jesus the Christ on the Greek island of Patmos. Suddenly, *from behind his back*, he hears a voice "loud as a trumpet-call" commanding him to write down what he sees in a book. We have already encountered that back-space from which the voice spoke to John. We recognized it as enclosing those beings and dimensions that vibrate on the etheric, emotional and spiritual levels of the soul. To "see whose voice it was," John had indeed to turn round and open up to his back-space. This means that he had to look through the eyes of his soul to be able to perceive the source of the voice: "On the Lord's day I knew myself inspired by the spirit, and I heard from behind me a voice loud as a trumpet-call, saying, 'Write down in a book what you see...' I turned to see whose voice it was speaking to me and when I had turned I saw..." (Rev 1:10 and 12)

What he saw first was the impersonal image of the seven golden candlesticks. They symbolize the cosmic consciousness which spreads the light of the spirit throughout the universe. That could be a sufficient image of God to satisfy any mind. But shortly afterwards John became aware of a personalized figure standing among the candlesticks. Here is his description: "He was dressed in a long robe with a golden girdle around his breast; his head and his hair were white as snow-white wool, his eyes blazed like fire, and his feet shone as the finest bronze glows in the furnace. His voice had the sound of a great waterfall, and I saw that in his right hand he held seven stars. A sharp two-edged sword came out of his mouth, and his face was ablaze like the sun at its height." (Rev 1:13)

My emotions start to sound an alarm when the principle of underlying wholeness takes on an anthropomorphic form. Is this God made in the image of a man? This is the point at which I would demand that we hold strictly to the discipline of understanding the images from Revelation as symbols, and not as depicting reality. So the seven stars can be understood as the love eternal and the sharp two-edged sword coming out of his mouth as the pure truth speaking. Both together, blending with "the sun at its height", are appropriate symbols to signify that here the reader has to do with the divine core of the universal consciousness.

But what does that mean for the universal consciousness to show itself in both an impersonal and a personalized image? It tells us that the consciousness of the universe is to be seen not only as the all-pervading vibration, but also as a point of self-awareness. It is that central point within the cosmic whole where the consciousness of the whole is aware of itself, creating purposefully and enjoying the creation consciously.

You will remember too that when the consciousness of the earth was under discussion, we talked about the involvement of at least two different levels. On one hand are elemental beings and nature spirits who embody different units and aspects of the earth's awareness. On the other there is the core, the all-embracing and self-aware consciousness that we call Mother Earth, or perhaps Gaia. And in this case there is a prevailing idea that the consciousness has a personal quality. It is aware of itself and of its creation. We tend to imagine it as having a human-like form because we know ourselves as self-conscious beings, and there is nothing else around that is tangible and visible and which we know to embody this special quality. So it comes about that the human form appears to be the proper symbol to clothe the self-conscious core of the cosmic awareness when it is about to reveal itself to human beings. It is the Divinity in person. To give it a name, John uses the term 'the Son of Man'. The Western tradition usually calls this face of divinity 'the Christ', which means 'the Anointed One'. The Eastern tradition would perhaps call it Buddha.

John continues: "When my eyes took in this sight I fell at his feet like a dead man. And then he placed his right hand upon me and said, 'Do not be afraid. I am the first and the last, the living one. I am he who was dead, and now you see me alive for time-less ages! I hold in my hand the keys of death and the grave'." (Rev 1:18) It is not by chance that John "fell at his feet like a dead man." Entering Revelation through the front door of the First Chapter, one encounters the Christ as a power abiding beyond the material plane on which people move during their incarnation in the web of daily life. They would experience the presence of the Christ as a reality only if they were to die. Stripped of the limitations of the one-dimensional world and freed from its limited perceptions, they could see his stature and listen to his voice as John did.

We should not overlook that the Christ presents himself as one who holds in his hand the keys of death and the grave. Indeed, following the laws of the 'old earth', dying to the physical life means being born again to the spiritual world. The Christ himself confirms to John that he had to die in order that he could be seen alive. Do we understand this properly? He had to die on the cross to pass through the gate of death. Only by passing through the gate of death could he become all-present, abiding everywhere within the spiritual realms of the earth and the universe.

As we know from history, the Christ incarnated approximately two thousands years ago in the person of Jesus of Nazareth, born within the Jewish culture. At that time, the Jewish religion's understanding of the cosmic whole was the most advanced of any in the Western hemisphere. It was focused on the core of God eternal, and was not lost in the hierarchies of innumerable divine beings and local cults.

It is a tragedy that Jewish culture in general, even though so advanced, was not able to accept the message that Jesus the Christ was preaching. The Jewish tradition was too deeply caught in its spiritual and emotional patterns that dictated a specific image of the 'Anointed One' and how he would appear among Jews, who saw themselves as the 'Chosen People'. The appearance of Jesus — a poor carpenter's son — did not conform to these fixed patterns. Coupled with the pragmatic rationality of the Roman civilization which was ruling Palestine at that time, Jewish conservatism was strong enough to 'kick' Jesus out of incarnation by way of crucifixion.

Yet the Gospel texts, which are the only documents to tell of his life, bear testimony that on the third day after being taken down from the cross, Jesus disappeared from his grave. Afterwards, he showed himself a few times to some individuals and to a group of his disciples in an etheric, close-to-material form. Only in the next phase, during the so-called Ascension, did he raise himself into the realms of spirit in front of his disciples' bewildered eyes.

If we enter the Book of Revelation by the front door, its message tells us that the most precious face of divinity, the self-consciousness of the universe in person, at one time walked among people. Later this precious divinity transcended death and is to be found and contacted at any time beyond the barriers of the material world, not only way up in the Heavens, but also in the nearby realms of the soul, on the other side of the threshold that divides the physical from the immaterial. This is the dimension which people have known since immemorial ages as the place where the deceased and our ancestors abide.

The most impassioned warnings are distributed throughout the whole Book of Revelation, urging people to be truthful, not to become 'liars, cowards, faithless and corrupt, murderers', etc. It urges us not to behave as if we were alone on the earth, doing whatever we want. It tells us, 'you cannot see it, but the divine presence is next to you — not in the lofty realms of spirit, but right there in the 'back-space' of your environment, supporting, observing and judging your deeds'. Never trust to the illusion that God is far away, especially not since he has incarnated in Palestine!

I have no problems either emotionally or ethically with such a vision of a nearby Divinity. I can agree to each detail. I am grateful, and ready to go on my knees and accept. It is only my intuition that tells me, ever since the earth's transmutation process got under way, that something essential is changing in the relationship between God, human beings and the earth cosmos. This notion first came to me in a dream. I dreamed it while working in Crete, Greece, during February 1999.

I dreamed that I was in my car on my way through France. This time, it was extremely difficult to drive on the French roads.

Again and again barricades that the police had put up stopped me. There was the idea that something was being transported which was very precious and it had to be made secure to the highest possible degree. Finally I got to know that the skull of Christ was being taken to Paris, to be exhibited there in a grand international show.

The next vision showed the skull of the Christ in the exhibition hall. It was placed within a glass cube, positioned in such a way that one could look into its empty brain-case through the aperture at its base. I noticed also that the skull was turned so that its gaze focused on the ceiling high above.

My first thought was that the dream's message was to make me aware of a chakra hidden beneath the base of the head. I spent half a year cradling this illusion because I didn't dare look at the horrifying truth that I sensed was underlying the vision. Only during my summer retreat on the small island in the Adriatic did I gather enough courage to attune properly to the quality behind the image. I was indeed shocked. I fell to the ground and could have cried and cried... I realized that the blasphemous transport of Christ's skull through the highways of France, and the shameless, public exhibition of its nakedness, were the symbolic marks of the end of an epoch most dear to my heart.

This was the epoch when we were building cathedrals, chanting in monasteries, praying with enthusiasm, inwardly in peace because we knew that the Christ was abiding next door in the invisible space all around us. We invented innumerable ways to communicate with him through art, ritual and selfless service. In effect, we became addicted to the notion that nothing could overthrow us since we were walking in the shadow of the Father.

We became self-confident; we started to manipulate theological assumptions, fight against their possible opponents, even kill ruthlessly in the name of the Cross. Later, we became more rational; we organized our institutions somewhat democratically and found legal ways to consolidate our positions of power. Do you wonder that the spiritual path towards which the 'front door' of the Book of Revelation is pointing has in the meanwhile become empty?

The vision of the empty skull has stripped me of my illusion that one's former relationship to the Christ, in the way he made possible by himself walking the path of death and resurrection, is still intact. 'Holding in his hand the keys of death', he made the effort to stay in the non-physical space closest to our reality, in the region beyond the grave[1]. I feel deeply grateful for the possibility he offered, but our human culture has manipulated it in a thousand ways and it has deteriorated into a kind of duality, where on the one hand we believe in God and on the other feel free to destroy nature or our fellow human beings. We have arrived at the limits of the spiritual growth that it can offer. That is the message of the empty skull: the Christ torn apart from the wholeness of his body and put on show in Paris.

As a result of the earth changes now in progress, the core of the universe is starting to abide by new principles to enable communication with the people of earth. To discover these, we have to take another door leading into the Revelation of St. John. Way back, I mentioned that the Apocalypse is an intricate constellation of two interlaced textual structures. One of them has a linear characteristic that starts at the official beginning of the Book and proceeds towards its end, in effect up to the image of the Last Judgment. The other one displays a spherical composition that emerges and expands from a vision positioned at the threshold of the 12th Chapter in the center of the book. From that point of entrance, the various chapters containing the visions of St. John are symmetrically arranged on both sides of an imaginary axis.

On the left hand side of the axis we have the 11th Chapter with the story of the *Two Witnesses*; on the right hand, the 13th Chapter containing the vision of the *Two Beasts*. The symmetry of the text becomes obvious when we continue looking to the left and right of the above-mentioned axis. The 10th Chapter starts with the image of '*a mighty angel* descending from Heaven', and on the other side, the 14th Chapter reveals the vision of '*another angel* flying in mid-heaven, holding the everlasting gospel'.

Continuing in the same fashion, in the 8th and the 9th Chapter we find the terrifying story of the *Seven Trumpets* which summon seven grievous disasters to strike the earth and its

1 Compare with my perception of the Christ presence during the ritual of the mass in *Christ Power and the Earth Goddess*, Chapter 1.

people. Its counterpart is to be found in the 15th Chapter on the other side of the axis. This tells the story of the *'seven last plagues'* which are to be poured out over the earth and its people. In effect, the seven disasters summoned by the trumpets are so destructive that, according to linear logic, there would be no need at all to supplement them with the seven plagues. Obviously, the plagues are needed only to maintain the spherical composition that is of such decisive importance for Revelation, by providing an alternative to the linear track that runs from the text's beginning to its end.

If we continue to read Revelation spherically, we find that the left hand side of the axis is rounded off by the Seven Letters to the Seven Churches. As already discussed, these portray the image of the renewed human being. The right hand side is similarly completed by the *seven qualities* of the New Jerusalem. Decoding them, we discovered that they symbolize the basic qualities of the renewed earth cosmos. The composition of Revelation is therefore notable not only for its clear symmetry but also for the spherical nature of its essence. At the 'end' of the text we find the image of the *new earth cosmos* — the New Jerusalem — which is complemented by the vision of the renewed *human being* at its 'beginning'. Both 'ends' are linked to each other so as to form a rounded whole.

This text, forming a fantastic spherical whole which embraces all in all, sprouts from one single seed planted in its midst, at the beginning of the 12th Chapter. It is the archetypal seed out of which all creation sprang: "Then a huge sign became visible in the sky — the figure of a woman clothed with the sun, with the moon under her feet, and a crown of twelve stars upon her head. She was pregnant, and cried out in her labor and in the pains of bringing forth her child." (Rev 12:1)

First of all one is surprised because the primal cause of creation is represented by a woman, not by the image of God. Yet there can't be any misunderstanding. The symbols denote clearly that it is she, the One who embodies all the three extensions of the universe. The crown of twelve stars upon her head stands for the cosmic dimension. Being clothed in the sun means that she also represents the powers of the solar system. Her standing on

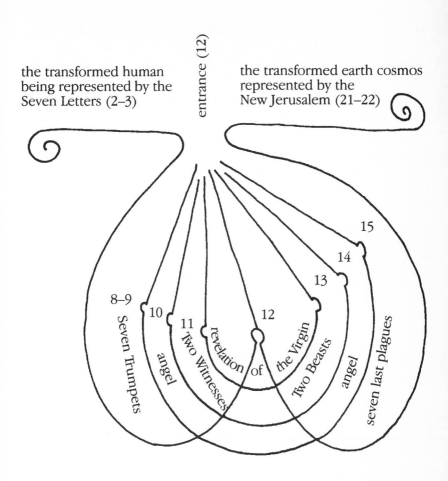

The spherical composition of the Revelation of St. John.
(Numbers denote relevant chapters of Revelation.)

the moon refers to the planetary dimension as her third domain, since the moon and the earth represent a holon.

One could call her the Universal Mother, or the Virgin, Mother of God. Being the nucleus around which evolves the whole spherical constellation of the cosmos, she is pregnant with the "male child who is to shepherd all the nations..." (Rev 12:5) Yet, so that she can spiritually hold in its place the tremendous power of the center, she is complemented by the cosmic counter-force, which is in tune with our discussion in the previous chapter. We have already got to know this force as the "serpent of the ancient times." The text of Revelation proceeds: "Then another sign became visible in the sky, and I saw that it was a huge red dragon with seven heads and ten horns, with a diadem upon each of his heads. His tail swept down a third of the stars in the sky..." (Rev 12:3) The image, "Sweeping down a third of the stars in the sky" refers to the proper cosmic proportions allocated between the powers of light and the powers of darkness, which we have already mentioned in discussing the wisdom of the Abbess Hildegard von Bingen.

So that the reader gets a feel for how fragile and ultimately dangerous is the equilibrium upon which life rests, Revelation continues: "The dragon took his place in front of the woman who was about to give birth to a child, so that as soon as she did so he might devour it. She gave birth to a male child who is to shepherd all the nations 'with a rod of iron'. Her child was snatched up to God and to his throne, while the woman fled into the desert..." (Rev 12:4) The moment that the powers which further evolution decided to take the next decisive forward step in the universal development of life, the sensitive equilibrium of life was obviously shaken. The Book of Revelation provides an image of how the powers of darkness tried to get rid of the 'male child' who would be the one to introduce this new step. He would embody it in his own life, lived in Palestine as Jesus the Christ. So his contemporaries, as I have already mentioned, forced the Christ out of incarnation. After only three years of public work, he was sent back where he came from, "snatched up to God and to his throne."

On September 16th 1999 I had a vision which gave me a glimpse of the nature of this new evolutionary step. I was sitting in a train that was carrying me through half of Europe towards Aachen, Germany, where I was to talk about my love for the Goddess. The journey started with some disastrous events that had a happy ending, so I was wondering what was to happen next. We were already traveling through the mountains of Austria when I noticed that I was sitting in the middle of a pillar of the finest golden rain. It continued and continued to fall, impregnating me with a unique feeling of tenderness and peace.

The silent voice of intuition started to talk to me, saying, "It is not by chance that so many pictures show Christ as a male child in the lap of his Mother. He came as a ray from other cosmic dimensions, to enter into our space through the heart of the Goddess. The Christ, depicted in the stature of a child, represents a different kind of vibration, one much more condensed than we have known hitherto. This is why his appearance as a small child is so characteristic: his smallness is relative, in tune with the concentrated kind of cosmic power which he embodies."

At that moment our train was running parallel to another. The other train was loaded with wooden boxes stamped in block letters with inscriptions saying: **super heavy**. I was reminded of the legend of St. Christopher, whose name in Greek means 'the carrier of Christ'. He was a giant who earned his living by carrying people across a wild river. One day a little 'male child' arrived at the bank and asked the giant to carry him across the waters. Nothing could be easier than that! But when he was carrying him, Christopher soon noticed that the child felt as heavy as if he were bearing the *whole world* on his shoulders.

The Book of Revelation is very clear about not giving a name either to the child or to the woman that gave birth to him. They both stand for primeval cosmic powers and not for consciousness. To be a small child and "to shepherd all the nations with a rod of iron" is a mighty symbol. Why is it not a rod of gold? Because the present stage of evolution is in a downward phase, descending from the level of 'gold' — equivalent to the regions of pure light — towards the 'age of iron'. From the heights of the spirit, the divine impulses are stepping down to the dense level of matter! The life which now bursts out on the etheric, emotional and spiritual levels must take on tangible forms, just as we know

*The legend of St. Christopher as depicted on the wall
of a medieval church in Carinthia, Austria.*

them from our earthly experience. It is to become the 'kingdom of Heaven upon the earth', as Jesus called it when he spoke to his disciples.

Look at all these stars and planets around us! How does it happen that all our sensitive apparatus, listening in to the universe, cannot detect any life in the earth's environment? Indeed, there may be none on the level on which we are searching, because the material level of existence belongs to the future phase of the universe. It is still waiting for its time to arrive. We are extremely lucky to be incarnate on the earth and already experiencing what, step by step, is about to become the overall reality of the future.

One can imagine that the new path with its hidden, unforeseen dangers put the opposing forces in a state of alarm, so the 'War in Heaven' started. In the last chapter I elaborated on the next portion of Revelation, in which 'Michael and his angels battled with the dragon'. (Rev 12:7) As you may remember, the dark forces were finally pushed down to the earth and obtained the cosmic permission to test — as severely as they wished – our human endeavor to transmit cosmic consciousness to the level of matter by embodying it in the form of tangible deeds.

If we wish to follow the 'small child' through his own evolution, leading beyond the task that he accomplished during his incarnation in Palestine, we have to go back to the spherical model of Revelation. One could compare it to the way our brain is organized, composed of two halves that are connected to each other across a central division. Listening to the right hemisphere of Revelation (Chapters 12 to 22) is like dealing with the right, or intuitive, half of the brain. There, one gets to know the feminine principle of divinity — the path of the Goddess. But if one moves to the left hemisphere (Chapters 12 to 1), which corresponds to the rational half of the brain, one can, by walking the path of the God, proceed to a more profound knowledge of the divine masculine principle. According to our theme, we should walk on this last path first.

Walking backwards, it will take us from the 12th to the 4th Chapter, which is entitled "The vision of Heaven." There we are told that "a throne had been set up in Heaven, and there was someone seated upon the throne. His appearance blazed like jasper and cornelian, and all around the throne shone a halo like an emerald rainbow. In a circle around the throne there were twenty-four thrones and seated upon them twenty-four elders dressed in white with golden crowns upon their heads. From the central throne come flashes of lightning, noises and peals of thunder. Seven lamps are burning before the throne, and they are the seven Spirits of God. In front of the throne there appears a sea of glass as clear as crystal. On each side, encircling the throne, are four living creatures covered with eyes in front and behind..." (Rev 4:2)

Here one is permitted to look at the workshop of the cosmic consciousness, equipped with all the kinds of tools needed to bring about the universal creation. Its core, symbolized by the central throne, is reserved for the self-conscious face of divinity. But this time it is not clothed in a post-mortem shape but presented as a formless light-body. The 24 elders represent the so-called 'ascended masters', women and men who in their personal development have reached enlightenment. They are capable of attuning to the impulses of the divine core and of coping with their purpose in order to further the divine cause. Next, we get to know the tools which are used to transform the impulses of the cosmic consciousness into deeds of creation:

• creative powers seen as flashes of lightening ...

• the seven Cosmic Rays symbolized through the seven lamps[2].

• the ether, as the primeval substance through which creation takes form, depicted as the sea of glass.

• the Four Elements denoting the four avenues through which the life-streams flow. They are symbolized by the four creatures, a lion, a calf, a third which "has a face like a man, and the fourth appears like an eagle in flight."

Yet it is only at the threshold of the Fifth Chapter that there is revealed the divine tool of most special importance and interest to us: "Then I noticed in the right hand of the One seated upon the throne a book filled with writing both inside and on its back, and

2 For information on the Seven Cosmic Rays, see Alice Bayley, *A Treatise on the Seven Rays*

it was sealed with seven seals. And I saw a mighty angel who called out in a loud voice, 'Who is fit to open the book and break its seals?'" (Rev 5:1) The book, filled with writing both inside and on its back, is the sealed book of future events. Usually, we would call it the original blueprint that guides the universal development. In the course of the past chapters we have carefully watched the opening of its seals, one after the other, and so have got to know the divine blueprint for the emerging earth cosmos.

We also took care to notice that the seals could not be opened if the Christ had not incarnated two thousand years ago and so united his cosmic powers with the powers of the earth. After going through the ritual death on the cross and completing his resurrection, he did not disappear from the earth. He proceeded with his mission for the planet by uniting with the elemental consciousness of the earth. This is why the Book of Revelation presents him in the form of an animal, the lamb that 'has been slaughtered' on the cross.

The lamb had "seven horns and seven eyes, which are the seven Spirits of God and are sent out into every corner of the earth." (Rev 5:6) The 'seven spirits of God sent out into every corner of the earth' is a most precious symbol. It tells us that the spirit of the Christ, abiding on the etheric plane of the planet, was not resting during the past two millennia while people were struggling to accept and understand the new role he had revealed for human beings. He was working to unite the cosmic impulses that he had brought to the planet with the consciousness of the earth. To put it symbolically, the seven divine spirits that he brought with him have been distributed 'into every corner of the earth'.

Whenever the divine presence takes the form of an animal — in our case a lamb — it stands for the incarnation of the divine within the organism of the earth. For at least forty thousand years the shamans of various cultures and epochs worldwide have contacted the spirits of different kinds of animals in order to approach the Divinity inherent within the earth cosmos. To bring knowledge and healing to the peoples of the earth, they had to travel spiritually to the otherworld and meet the animal spirits there. Younger cultures later developed the mediating roles of priests and gurus to be able to stay in touch with the Divine. And today, priests of different orientations are facilitating the approach to the Christ presence.

In contrast to these two traditional ways of communicating with the Divinity, the Revelation of St. John offers the revolutionary vision of the male aspect of Divinity involved in the process of change. The process starts with the little boy sitting in the lap of the universal Mother, where he represents the ever-new divine impulse that inspires the evolution of the cosmic creation. In the next phase of transformation, Revelation depicts the divine presence as the throne of creation, representing the creative knowledge and power of the universal consciousness, out of which stars, planets and flowers are everlastingly being called into existence.

The lamb represents the third phase of God[3] when he is making the Heavens tangible by stepping down into the multidimensional space of the earth cosmos to merge with its power fields and its consciousness. No techniques are needed now to communicate with Divinity, nor is there need of any intermediaries. The third phase makes possible an astonishing co-existence with the Divine. The words of Revelation express this new relationship, made possible through the changes occurring within the earth cosmos and within the human being: "See the home of God is with men, and he will live among them. They shall be his people, and God himself shall be with them, and will wipe away every tear from their eyes." (Rev 21:3)

This is not a promise of a distant happy future, as is often believed. The text testifies to the fantastically contradictory nature of the divine consciousness: present within each particle of the universe while simultaneously embracing its whole, and even – considering the third phase of Divinity – both incarnate and pure spirit in the same moment of eternity.

Rather than a promise of a distant future, it is a call to develop such a spiritual practice on the personal and group levels as will enable the third phase of Divinity to become reality. The following chapter offers some proposals that I developed during the years 1998-99, after I had become aware that the changing earth cosmos demands a complementary spiritual engagement on our part.

3 Traditionally, the third phase of God is symbolised by another animal, the dove.

Chapter Nine

Meditations and Ritual Patterns to Support Personal and Earth Changes

Just a few days after I had had the terrible vision of the skull of Christ put on show in Paris, a dream brought home to me the need to intuit a personal spiritual practice which was in tune with the changing earth cosmos. In the dream I saw myself traveling around the world, from lecture to lecture and from workshop to workshop, and always carrying with me an awful lot of luggage. I often had to struggle with the problems of transporting it, like looking for people to help me carry the pieces that I couldn't manage with my two hands, and so on. But after a while I noticed that there was a kind of alternative luggage that accompanied me wherever I went. At first I thought it was a new patent device, invented by a travel goods company, which its managers wanted to sell to me. So I would ignore it.

One day I was curious and — while nobody was looking — I stopped to examine the alternative luggage. It had all been packed on a small two-wheeled wagon made of iron, such as porters use on railway stations. Using my two hands, I could move it easily. I was especially amazed that such a small amount of luggage could contain everything that one could possibly need on a long journey. To feel the quality of its contents, carefully tied together with cord, I took out a jacket and put it on. Again I was surprised by the high quality of the fabric and its fashionable design. Then I opened a small, neat box and realized that many different sorts of the very best chocolate were packed within. But I didn't allow myself to taste them because my mother had taught me not to eat chocolate before my main meal!

First of all the dream made me aware that my psyche was still nurturing barriers which blocked the fantastic freedom in spiritual and religious practice which is offered us by the transforming earth cosmos. In times past, we were much more dependent on forces and mediators from the outside to guide our human spiritual paths. By 'outside', I mean the cosmic dimensional framework, i.e., the ancestors, ascended masters and angelic beings, and the occasions when people tended to listen rather blindly to their guidance; and also the human cultural framework, i.e., priests, gurus and spiritual leaders in their mediating roles, when they advanced their preconceived or dogmatically fixed patterns of belief without giving individuals the freedom to choose and decide according to the senses of their own hearts.

The dream was advising me to cut back on my spiritual and religious 'luggage' to the amount that in any given moment would really help me forward on my personal spiritual path. Of course, one might need some other kind of tool to take another step on the next phase of the path. So you should feel free to choose whatever new tools inspire you, and not hesitate to free yourself from a specific spiritual practice if you discover — by listening carefully within — that its patterns have become a drag on your further development. The conditions that are emerging in the transforming, changing earth cosmos demand a dynamic, non-dogmatic and flexible spiritual practice.

For the past two years I have been constantly attuning to the surprising twists and turns in the flow of the earth changes I have been describing. I have tried to follow them through my own spiritual practice and through the way I work with groups. In what follows, I offer some examples in the hope that they can be useful to you on your own spiritual journey. Perhaps they can inspire you to find some new solutions for yourself. The hologrammic-touch exercises can also be useful for personal or group attunement.

Meditation patterns for personal or group practice

1. *Talk to the child within*

To go 'backward' to the sources of your being, simply sit down peacefully and imagine yourself to be a small child who is taken onto your lap. If you do this with confidence and an open heart, any illusions or mental preconceptions will instantly be stripped away. And if your attitude is one of love and inner peace, it will bring you straight to the source of truth. Feel free to listen to yourself as you are. Let your soul vibrate beyond any of the patterns and norms that culture, parents and education have projected onto you in the course of your development.

I also use this kind of meditation whenever I am unsure whether I am relating to a true reality, or whether I am perhaps subordinating myself to some trickster illusion. In such cases I observe the reactions of the child on my lap. These are a sure guide. I use the same method to help myself out when perception is difficult, as when I am confronted with places whose character has been suppressed and in consequence are holding to certain patterns mimicking the past.

2. *The circle and its center*

It is important to do this exercise again and again to get in tune with one of the basic principles of the renewed earth cosmos: connecting opposites in a way that transcends all logic. This means embodying the powers of synergy. The following meditation is a simple way to work on this:

Find your inner peace and concentrate on the innermost center of your heart. While continuing to hold your center, spread your consciousness outward, to finally encompass the complete sphere of the cosmos in all its vastness. For a while, keep your attention simultaneously focused both on the vast circle of the whole and on its center in your heart also.

3. The triple tree

The next experience is the joining of the earthly and cosmic dimensions to give birth to a new unity, which I usually call the earth cosmos. Human beings could act as the bridge to make this interlacing of earth and cosmos into a living reality. One of the meditations I use for this purpose is called 'The Triple Tree'.

1.Imagine that you are a tree firmly rooted in the earth, with your branches reaching high into the sky to touch the stars. The saps of life eternal are flowing through you to be exchanged by earth and heaven.

2. Then imagine that the branches of the same tree are actually its roots, and you are making the roots become its branches. As a soul-being you are indeed coming from the stars, to open the blossoms of your love towards the center of the earth (which can be imagined as the heart of the Earth Mother).

3. When, from the core of the earth, the response reaches you, make it into a light-body of the Tree of Life which grows through you towards the Heavens.

These three transformations of the same tree can also represent the three aspects of human grounding; demonstrating our energetic, emotional and spiritual oneness with the earth cosmos.

4. Experience the quality of the earth consciousness

This meditation, which can also be used as a guided meditation for groups, is designed so that one glides through the experience of the Four Elements to arrive at the core consciousness which unites them and which is the self-consciousness of the Earth. It was given to me as inspiration, after I had asked the Earth to show me how to lead a group of students to experience her core.

1. Imagine that you are walking slowly through an endless avenue where beautiful old trees are growing on either side. After a while you notice a gust of wind that suddenly comes from the side to play around you and then disappears. (The presence of the Element Air)

2. You continue to walk down the avenue, and at one point enter a belt of milky white fog which extends right across between the trees. You can feel the tiny drops of water all around you. (The presence of the Element Water)

3. You still continue walking down the avenue and leave the belt of fog way behind you. Now you approach a glade where the crowns of the trees open out to allow the rays of bright solar light to enter the shadowy space of the avenue. You enter the area lit by the sun's rays and enjoy their warmth. (The presence of the Element Fire)

4. Now you come to the end of the avenue where you find a gigantic rock wall 'growing' out of the earth. But surprisingly, the path you have been following does not stop at the foot of the rock. There is a natural tunnel leading right into its heart. When you walk into the tunnel, the light becomes dimmer and dimmer and you soon find yourself in complete darkness, surrounded by the powerful feel of rocks all around you. (The presence of the Element Earth)

5. Do not stay there, but continue to walk consciously through the darkness which is becoming less dense, illumined more and more by an unknown source of dim blue light at the other end of the tunnel. Now you reach its exit and step into a vast underground chamber lit by the same bluish, semi-bright light coming from its floor and walls.

6. Stay for a while in this inner chamber of the earth and try to feel its quality. It is the quality of the earth's core, something which frightens people and they consequently tend to ignore it. Then become aware of the core of your heart, which is in tune with the heart of the earth. After a while you should identify with the heart of the universe and lift yourself into oneness with the cosmic whole. Now you are back home and can open the eyes.

5. The Little Red Riding Hood meditation

The folk tales coming from the area of the Meissner Mountain in central Germany, which were written down by the brothers Grimm, are a treasury of the profoundest wisdom. Two chapters back I was referring to the story of the Sleeping Beauty[1].

---

1 Two other tales from the Grimm-collection play important role in my other books: Snow White in *Healing the Heart of the Earth* (Part 3, Chapters 4 and 5) and Cinderella in the 13th Chapter of *Christ Power and the Earth Goddess*. I do not refer to the Walt Disney versions, which can be very different from the originals!

While I was researching our culture's relationship with the world of the ancestors, another famous tale from the Brothers Grimm repertory knocked on the door of my consciousness: Little Red Riding Hood.

It tells of a young girl named Little Red Riding Hood who went through a dark forest to visit her grandmother. The deep forest in whose midst the grandmother lived symbolizes the otherworld where the ancestors abide and take care of the wisdom and knowledge of eternity. The girl who went to visit her grandmother, bringing her a basket full of red strawberries, represents the ancient people who used to walk the ritual paths to places where they could contact the ancestors — we have described such a place at Hoga in Sweden. The basket full of strawberries is a symbol of the ritual gifts they brought with them.

But the wolf, as a symbol of the dark powers, saw the approaching girl, ran to the grandma's house, devoured her and put on her clothes and spectacles. Lying in her bed and answering Little Red Riding Hood's questions, he was deceiving the girl in order to ultimately devour her also.

The Little Red Riding Hood story is a tale of warning. It tells people of our modern era that the spiritual paths that folk, very respectfully, used to walk to contact their ancestors have in the meanwhile been occupied by destructive forces and possibly misused. Merely by wanting to listen to the wisdom of the underworld, one could be seduced by the voices of some astral demons[2].

The meditation proposed here accords with the message of the Fourth Seal. It is meant to reverse the negative pattern that the tale of Little Red Riding Hood imprints on the subconscious of incoming generations. The self-healing powers of the transforming earth cosmos have cleared the sullied paths and made possible a new level of contact with the dimensions of the world soul and the ancestors.

1. Close your eyes and imagine that you are a little girl who is skipping through a beautiful forest to visit your grandmother.

2. Arriving at the clearing in the middle of the forest, you

2 For questions about 'astral demons', see my book *Healing the Heart of the Earth*, Part 4.

find a small house. You open the door and whom do you see sit-ting comfortably in the armchair? Your grandma! She embraces you happily and together you sit in the doorway of her house gazing into times past and future...

3. At that point you open your heart and mind and let the spirit guide you to explore whatever is standing by you right then ready for investigation. Feel free to put questions, and listen to the answers.

6. *Meditation to caress a selected place, landscape or country with love and support*

1. Center yourself in your heart, close your eyes, and imag-ine that you are standing in the very middle of the place, land-scape or country whose life-quality or health you wish to sup-port.

2. Then slowly lift the place, landscape or country, which now extends all around you, to the level of your heart.

3. Imagine how the different parts of the chosen place, land-scape or country have their source in the powers of your heart, even if geographically they lie far away. In your imagination go from one to another and caress them with your love. All the time, be aware that you are holding them tight in the center of your heart.

7. *Meditation to blend light and darkness*

1. Center yourself in your heart, close your eyes and in your imagination re-create the beautiful sunlight surrounding you, just as it usually shines on you.

2. Carry all that light into the inner space of your body and imagine that dark night is now all around you, with tiny stars twinkling in the distance.

3. Hold both visions present at the same time: the light shin-ing inside centered in your heart, and the darkness all around you.

4. After a while, release this image and start to explore the depths of your heart space.

I have mentioned that there were two especially difficult phases in the process of the earth changes, one in the first half of 1999 and the other in the month of transition between 1999 and 2000. Each time, my daughter Ana Pogacnik asked the angelic world what would be the best way for individuals or groups to help. Both the following meditations (8 & 9) continue to be valid ways of helping smooth the process of earth changes. I offer them here in the same order that they came into being.

8. Meditation to link earth and cosmos

1. Build a crystal-white channel from your heart towards the center of the earth and let the earth energies flow through this channel into your body.

2. Build a similar channel towards the cosmic realms and let cosmic energy flow down to fill your body.

3. Connect both energy flows in your heart-space, braiding them together so that they become a harmonious whole.

4. Go into your heart — if you are working as a group, build a network of heart-connections within the group — and imagine light bridges connecting you worldwide with the other individuals and groups who are dedicated to the powers of light, love and peace.

5. Now imagine that the light stream within your vertical channel is bright with different colors and reinforced by the power of your heart. Let the stream flow vividly upwards and downwards and broaden it to encompass the whole planet.

6. Then take the planet in your hands and put it into your heart space. Wrap it and embrace it with different colors and become one with it.

7. Afterwards imagine the opposite, that it is you who are standing within the heart of the earth, embraced by its presence and its colors. From the depth of your being, become one with the planet.

8. Stay centered in your heart for a while, holding the earth within it wrapped in the color green (the color of the heart), and imbued with the power of the Four Elements. Be open to the angelic presence and to the power of other beings of love.

9. *One can conclude by singing in harmonious tones, which distributes the concentrated energies, or simply by staying for a while as an open channel.*

9. Light axis meditation

This is the second meditation which Ana channeled on December 13th 1999:

1. Relax into inner peace and attunement. Connect with the rainbow-colored web of individuals and groups who are participating in the work of light, love and peace.

2. Imagine the light axis that is vibrating through you, connecting the cosmic realms with the center of the earth, and feel its presence.

3. Become aware of your personal force field and feel its openness. Then become aware of the force field of the earth and imagine that both are converging, the one flowing into the other. Keep the feeling of their unity firmly in your consciousness for a while.

4. Within this united force field, be aware of your physical body as if it were part of the earth body. Let yourself become the earth, and fill this united whole with light and the whole spectrum of colors.

5. Now be aware that you are a channel, a pillar of light or an axis going deep down to the center of the earth, down to the point where we all our light pillars are anchored. Centered in the core of the earth, see the star-like pattern through which all the people of the earth are connected (see drawing).

6. Go with the power of your heart and with your light into the core of the earth, down to the point where all of us are united, and help that point become a shining star.

7. One can close by singing harmoniously in support of the power of the star which links all human beings to the center of the earth and increasingly is shining out into the universe.

Ritual patterns for group work

I love group work because it has synergetic powers and makes bonds that vibrate between the individuals involved. In practice, there are two forms. In the first, a group comes together physically, in the second they are scattered spatially but telepathically attuned as a group to the same timeframe and common purpose. As a first step, I would like to give some examples of how I work with the groups which come together to do geomantic work related to the process of the earth changes.

1. Establishing a group

To ensure that the work of a group is in tune with the new powers and qualities of the earth, I always start its ritual work with the personal grounding and protection exercises already mentioned, and in addition, with some of the hologrammic touch gestures. The group then forms a circle with the participants standing close together, and we proceed to establish the group. The method we use for linking with each other comes from the hologrammic touch exercises taught me by the Minoan culture from Crete:

1. Stand close together in a circle and see that women and men are rhythmically distributed throughout. Each person puts their left hand on the lower back of the person to their left — just above the buttocks — and their right hand on the right shoulder of the person to their right. In this way a rhythmical yin-yang (shadow-light) link is formed on the energy level.

2. Standing like this, the group should connect lovingly from heart to heart in an anti-clockwise direction. This connects the group on the emotional level.

3. Finally, all should imagine that the group is standing within a sphere of crystal-white light, representing the group holon. Now the coming together is complete on the spiritual level.

2. Attuning a place or landscape to the new powers and qualities

There are some places and landscapes which are so over-loaded with their cultural functions that they simply cannot follow the natural course of the earth changes. They are trapped in the different kinds of patterns and bonds that people have projected onto them. Our purpose should be to free such places or land-scapes from these bonds and give them a chance to get connected to the flow of earth changes. If people have caused the problems, people should help solve them.

During our workshop at Findhorn, Scotland, in June 1999, I asked my daughter Ajra Miska to make contact with her angel master and ask him to suggest how a group could help a place or landscape become attuned to the course of the earth changes. In what follows, I set forth some of the ritual patterns that the angel proposed. Be creative and alter them according to your own inspiration if you feel so inclined.

1. Start with personal grounding and connecting. Then link as a group, as outlined above.

2. Form a circle, holding hands, and start by attuning the place to the qualities of the Four Elements. The leader of the ritual should call the Elements into the circle one after the other:

- *feel wind and spiraling breezes within the circle (Element Air)*
- *see flames of fire dancing within the circle (Element Fire)*
- *imagine that the ground within the circle grows into a mound of earth (Element Earth)*
- *imagine that as a circle you are forming a bowl which is being filled with water (Element Water)*

3. Let the water flow out to bless the environment. The leader now states aloud the purpose of the work. She or he briefly describes the spiritual or geomantic identity of the place with which the group is working. The beings of the Four Elements, and angelic beings too, are to be invited to help with the work.

4. Now a ritual invoking the identity of the place or landscape must be performed. It can be done in many different ways. Let me propose some:

- *all standing in a circle, visualize that the cosmogram of the place or landscape is emerging out of the earth within the circle and floating for a while above the ground,*
- *all go into the circle that has been formed and stamp on the ground, building up a rhythmical pattern; take your time so that the proper pattern can emerge, This will dissolve the circle.*
- *design a dance that is in tune with the place or landscape you are working with, etc.*

     5. Form the circle again and stand peacefully for a while so as to give the place an opportunity to calm down and re-order itself. Otherwise the change could trigger confusion.

     6. Close by thanking the beings of nature for their help.

3. Attuning elemental beings to the new powers and qualities

     The centers of elemental beings can also be trapped in strange patterns. After one has clarified the kind of problem that is disturbing them, help may be offered through the following ritual:

     1-2. Steps one and two can be performed as above. Or if a variation is desired, the group can attune to the Four Elements through the presence of the Elements within their own bodies, using the following pattern:

- *Element Air: the group breathes consciously for a while,*
- *Element Fire: participants attune to the pulsation of the blood in their veins,*
- *Element Earth: the group attunes to the firmness of the physical body,*
- *Element Water: participants listen to the circulation of the life power through their bodies.*

     3. The leader of the ritual salutes the elemental beings of the place, explaining in a few words the purpose of the work, and invites them to use the ritual circle as a door to enter our world.

     4. With invisible threads of different colors, the group starts to weave a rainbow-colored membrane from heart to heart.

While 'weaving' the membrane, each participant should call on the elemental beings concerned, or the relevant consciousness, to pass through the membrane to become attuned.

5. The group holds the membrane anchored in their hearts, singing in harmonious tones for a while to help the elemental consciousness during its process of gliding through the rainbow threads. All through this time, keep the feeling of love focused at the elemental level.

6. Conclude by giving thanks.

4. Renewing the dedication of a sacred place

During the past centuries many sacred places have been destroyed, estranged through wrong use or simply forgotten. In her process of transmutation, Earth will need many of these places in order to move forward in her dance of transformation. They need to be 'given to her', so that they can take over new roles within the corresponding landscape temple. We performed the following ritual for the first time at Blackhills near Elgin, Scotland, with Ajra and the Findhorn workshop group. It goes like this:

1. The group connects in a circle as outlined above.

2. The participants become aware of their personal role as an antenna operating between earth and cosmos.

3. The leader of the ritual asks aloud that the place be newly dedicated, and states the role and quality for which the place is aiming.

4. The group visualizes a pillar of light that connects the center of the circle with the cosmic heights.

5. The circle of participants should understand that they represent the outer fringe of the pillar of light and are acting as the medium between the blessing descending the pillar and the environment that is to be blessed with the new dedication. The group should imagine itself as a corona of light shining into the surrounding ambience.

6. While all are standing like this, the leader of the ritual starts to sing in harmonious tones. The person to his or her left joins in, and in this way a harmonious tune builds up, and moves in a clockwise direction.

7. When the singing has ended and there is silence, the group should release each other's hands, dropping them to their sides to open the circle; the participants should then move their hips in the form of a lemniscate – the sign of infinity — to invoke angelic blessings on the place.

5. Comforting the animal kingdom

In August 1999, when I was preparing a workshop at the Wassermann Zentrum (Aquarius Center) at Stuttgart, Germany, I unexpectedly got into conversation with the deva of the nearby forest. She urged me to perform a work which would comfort the animals who are, as we all know, extremely badly treated by the present civilization[3]. She showed me how to do it, as follows:

1. Select a place that is dear to animals, one where they choose to convene, or come regularly to drink water.

2. The participants choose their places within the ambience, close their eyes and each attunes, for him or herself, to the place and to the animal kingdom.

3. Then each participant should put their hands together in their lap so that the middle fingers touch each other to form a kind of a seat. Each one should then silently invite an animal to jump into this seat. Be aware what kind of animal comes to you, so that after the ritual you can share your experience with the others.

4. While holding the (invisible) animals in their laps, the group should sing harmoniously so as to create a channel for the flow of universal love to caress the animal kingdom.

5. When the singing is over, everyone opens their hands wide so that the animals can jump back into the ethers.

---

3 Chapter 7 of *Elemental Beings and Nature Spirits* is also devoted to the role of animals.

6. Telepathic group work to revitalize places, landscapes and countries

If a group wishes to work on some place with larger dimensions than can be handled within a circle, it is possible to split into smaller groups. Each goes to the places appointed to them and there they will perform the ritual work simultaneously. The places where each of the small groups are to work and the exact time of the ritual must be known to the whole group. I learned this exciting method of telepathic group work from my colleague Johanna Markl when, together with Stefan Brönnle, we were leading an education course in geomancy and earth healing in Germany. The following is my way of creating the telepathic form of group work:

1. The purpose of the work must be explained to the group as a whole, and the separate places presented where the small groups will work simultaneously. A schedule must be created so that all the groups will perform the same parts of the ritual at the same time. And of course there must be a fixed time to start the ritual at the different locations.

2. A group attunement then follows. Afterwards, the main group splits into small groups and these go to the places selected.

3. When the groups have all arrived at their places and the agreed starting time is approaching, each individual begins with a personal attunement — perhaps using hologrammic touch exercises — and also attunes to the place itself. Shortly before the ritual is due to begin, each group forms a circle and they attune as a group.

4. At the agreed starting time, each of the groups begins by building a light bridge to each of the other groups involved in the work so as to make a telepathic link with all of them, following the previously agreed time-schedule. To coordinate group visualization, each group leader should call out, in sequence, the names of the places selected. Participants should visualize a light bridge being built from their group down into the depths of the earth, and from there up to the place corresponding to the name which has been called out. From that place they visualize a backward stream of light leading to the place where they are standing. Each link should be kept active for a while.

5. *When the link has been made, the group can proceed with the ritual previously agreed. This can be a dance, a song or a set of hologrammic touch exercises.*

6. *Close the work by singing in harmonious tones.*

7. *Afterwards, each participant should make enough time to listen to the place or landscape where they have been working, so as to realize what processes the ritual has put in motion, or what images have arisen after its performance. Each person's experience should be later exchanged with the group as a whole when it comes together again.*

A large work of this kind was performed on the eve of the solar eclipse on August 11th 1999. On that evening 85 groups, distributed in selected places across Europe and Brazil, simultaneously carried out a ritual work to reconnect and rededicate the landscape temple of Europe and ensure its incorporation into the greater whole of the landscape temple of the Atlantic. The groups were not distributed randomly, but were located only in those places where I had, together with the local population, performed earth purification and healing work over the past seven years.

Inspiration for simultaneous group work on the landscape temple of Europe[4] had made itself felt for the first time in February of the same year, during the healing work which Ana and I were conducting on Crete. We had got to know Crete as a kind of root chakra of Europe, the place where the knowledge of the whole cultural evolution of the continent is stored. The next step, that of discovering the axis around which the light-body of Europe is arranged, was initiated by the new wave of tragic events taking place in the territory of the former Yugoslavia. The urgent need to integrate the Balkans, the rejected 'belly', into the totality of Europe came once again to the fore after the war around Kosovo was internationalized in Spring 1999, and NATO's bombing of Serbia started.

If Crete represents the root chakra of Europe, then, following the backbone of the continent northwards, the Balkans would

---

4 The concept of how landscape temples represent the spiritual dimension of the earth will be explained in the following Chapter.

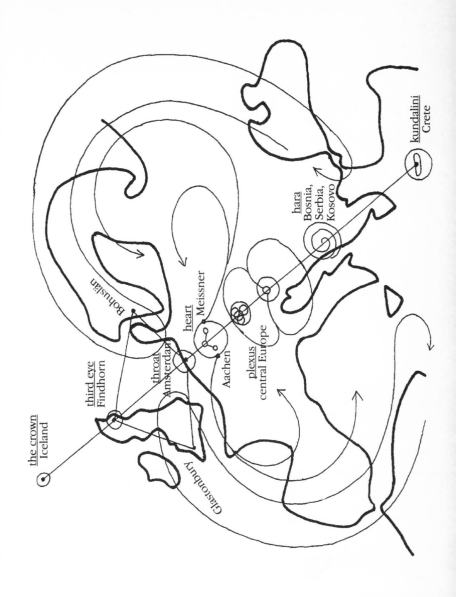

The landscape temple of Europe, on the reconnection and rededication of which the groups were working on the eve of the solar eclipse of August 11th 1999.

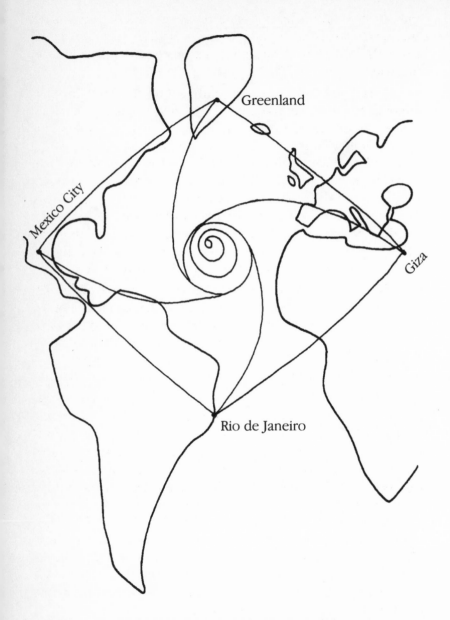

The landscape temple of the Atlantic,
corresponding to the one of Europe.

embody its vital functions, a kind of sexual chakra. The original European culture was born there in the Neolithic era and spread across the continent. It was a matrilineal culture, full of life and creativity.

The central European area south and north of the Alps corresponds to the function of the solar plexus chakra. It is centered around the Chiemsee Lake where Europe's vital energy center is located. Following the axis further north, the heart center would be found in the northern part of Central Europe, in the area between Aachen and Kassel (Meissner mountains) in Germany. The landscape temple which extends between Amsterdam, Glastonbury, Findhorn and Bohuslän in Sweden – when compared to the light-body of the human being — corresponds to the joint functions of the throat and third eye chakras. One should look to Iceland in the North Atlantic for the crown chakra.

If you look at my drawing of the landscape temple of Europe, you will see that to the left and right of its 'backbone' there are other landscape temples which extend to complement the light-body of Europe as a whole. My perception suggests that the light-body of the continent is not flat but has a spherical form, composed of different layers 'rotating' around the axis I have described.

Based on my experience of several years of earth healing work in Brazil and Mexico, I could go even further. While preparing for the work on August 10th, I did for a moment perceive that the landscape temple of Europe is only a fractal of a much larger light-body which encompasses the Atlantic Ocean. Its form is made up of two triangles. Two sides of the northern triangle connect the backbone of Europe with the eastern shores of the USA. The southern triangle connects Africa with South America. There exists a similar polarity between the two triangles as between Western Europe and the Balkans. The northern triangle is mentality-ruled and progress-orientated, the southern one bursts with vital powers and emotional intensity.

This differentiation between the two triangles of the Atlantic ambience, as it makes itself manifest on the economic, political and cultural levels, conceals a fantastic synergetic potential if properly understood and balanced. The purpose of the joint work of the groups on the eve of the solar eclipse of August 11th was primarily to help stabilize and re-connect the dismembered parts of the planetary landscape temples involved in the Atlantic ambience. Continuation of similar ritual work will be needed in future, to support and help prosper the conscious efforts of groups and individuals worldwide to cooperate with the processes of the changing earth. While I am writing this book, the groups in Europe are taking steps to create an international Lifeweb for Geomancy and Transformation, and this should offer possibilities for such a joint venture.

Chapter Ten

The Art of Living —
The Path of the Goddess

Our contemplation of the present cycle of earth changes and related human transformation is coming to a close. We started by considering the most down-to-earth phenomena, i.e., the changes that were occurring in the rhythms of ground radiation, and afterwards pursued the succession of the Seven Seals of the Apocalypse to see how the process of earth's transmutation runs on many different levels. Then, in the 8th Chapter we started to meditate upon the sacred dimensions of life and to consider the possibility that in the context of the earth's transformation, they would also change.

All the dimensions of life are in their own way sacred, but there is one in particular which we are accustomed to consider as specifically holy because it denotes Divinity, and refers to the spiritual background of the cosmos, and the sacred extensions of nature and landscape too. Traditionally, we speak of it as the spiritual dimension, or refer it to different religious practices. Yet all too often – both in the traditional religions and in modern spiritual movements — the religious belief systems or spiritual aspirations tend to be lifted out of the web of life and made to constitute a kind of guiding and directing mechanism that works from the outside to govern the flow of life.

This tendency to extrapolate one aspect out of the whole and allot it a preeminent place is in direct opposition to the quality of interconnectedness that we have recognized as one of the basic properties of the emerging earth cosmos. Interconnectedness is the golden thread which has guided my understanding of what the earth's transformation process is all about. Did I not express it clearly enough throughout this book? Just as one should decisively reject the idea that any, even the most frightful, manifestations of life should be excluded from its totality, so one should also persistently affirm that there should be no exalted layer of religious or spiritual superstructures floating above life's web.

To make the image of a Divinity that is fully integrated into life's web less ideological and more tangible, I would like to narrate a dream that I received on January 20, 1999. It started with the news that a most exciting sanctuary had been found intact right in the middle of Belgrade, Serbia, the city that nowadays bears the stamp of dictatorship and the cruelty associated with the wars in the Balkans. I wondered how was it possible that nobody had ever noticed the sanctuary before? I immediately started out to visit it. Arriving there, I was even more amazed to see that the exterior of the sanctuary was built most impressively in the form of a conical pyramid, each of its several stories decorated in a different style. Surprisingly, it fitted perfectly among the banal facades of the adjacent houses

But when you enter the sanctuary in my dream, you find yourself in a family kitchen with little children around, and you are looking at the normal, everyday life which goes in kitchens. To my surprise, the stove that the family used for cooking was also the altar of the sanctuary. But then I noticed that even though the place looked so common, you had to pass two barriers made of the finest white marble to approach the altar/stove. The first one was placed so very low that you had to crawl under it, touching the earth with your whole body. The second one was positioned higher so that a visitor would have to jump over it. Another surprise hit me when I noticed that the people who belonged to the family simply went through the barriers as if these consisted of pure spirit and not of marble. They didn't have to bow down or jump.

At that moment I became overexcited and ran to a friend's house to tell him about the exquisite find. My mind invented a whole story about how the sanctity of the place was due to its location close to an important historical site. But when, with my friend in tow, I arrived back at the place where the sanctuary was, I could find neither its door nor its impressive facade. I began to run around searching, till eventually I found somebody who promised to lead me to it. Following him, I got the idea that he was leading me astray. Still I stayed latched onto him as my last hope of ever finding the sanctuary again. But while I was distracted for an instant, the stranger disappeared behind a door. There were many doors, and I opened one hoping to catch him, but it was the wrong door... I was lost.

Going over the dream in my mind, I realized first of all that the message was directed at the illusions I was nurturing about the sacred dimensions of life. I expected the newly emerging sanctity of the earth to manifest in special, highly interesting forms that are unknown to us today. This expectation of discovering new religious and spiritual patterns was leading me astray and causing me to lose the connection to the true sacred quality of the manifesting earth cosmos. In contrary fashion, the message of the dream was bringing to the fore the surprising vision of the sacred and spiritual dimension 'impregnated' within the tissue of normal life. Yet there was a clear distinction made between that and the chaotic and distracted way of life we know today. It is symbolized by the two barriers made of the finest white marble. They demand that anybody wishing to participate in the dance of life should pass through a kind of initiation, though not a formal one. If there were a formal threshold demanding that people bow to certain preconditions or dogmas, then the people living within the surprising fusion of family house and temple could not pass freely through the barriers as if they did not exist. The context of the dream shows clearly that the barriers are there only to challenge those who approach the new quality of life from the outside.

The two barriers represent the initiation which is the precondition for one's ability to participate in the sacred quality of the life which is now manifesting within the renewed earth cosmos. One has to prostrate oneself down to the earth to be able afterwards to 'fly' across the second white marble barrier. It could be defined as an initiation that requires the human being to go through the extreme fragmentation demanded by the diversity of possibilities on the earthly plane of existence, and yet simultaneously stay rooted in the cosmic wholeness.

This is not a symbolic 'initiation' but a very practical one that needs to be practiced every day, because it refers to the flow of life itself. I would identify it with the path of the Goddess. The time has come to detach ourselves from our culture's obsession with a singular relationship with God and aim for more balance on all levels – and especially when we are concerned with the highest principles of existence. To find an entryway to the sacred dimension of the earth cosmos, it is not enough for us to relate in a new way to the impulse-imparting male aspect of Divinity. We also need to know the life-enhancing presence of the Goddess. I believe that there is no way around this.

Western culture is always inventing new reasons to avoid meeting the Goddess. To consider the feminine aspect of Divinity as equally important as the masculine is often identified with paganism — as if one were making out of one God, two. On the other hand, feminine qualities are ascribed to the male God as part of his all-embracing nature. This makes a 'valid' excuse to eliminate any need to open up to the reality of the Goddess. But why not look at it from the opposite point of view and devote our attention first to the Goddess principle, and then see how the masculine counterpart fits into the wholeness that she represents? This is exactly the way in which the Revelation of St. John has structured the proportions of its text, so as to stimulate a new quality of relationship with the divine core of the universe. Let us listen to its proposals.

We have already worked out the details of how the Apocalypse represents a spherical composition of visions and insights centered around the revelation of the Goddess. I am here referring to the 12th Chapter and the moment when "a huge sign became visible in the sky — the figure of a woman clothed with the sun, with the moon under her feet, and a crown of twelve stars upon her head. She was pregnant, and cried out in her labor and in the pains of bringing forth her child."

The image of the Virgin, representing the wholeness of the universe, is a mighty archetype that belongs to the ageless memory of all cultures. To get to know this archetype in all its facets, one has to follow the symmetrical path of Revelation as it evolves out of the central vision of the Virgin. Taking this path, we get to

The Virgin Goddess with her Divine Son
from the bronze-age culture of northern Greece.

know, one after the other, all the different attributes of the Goddess as they are known from her ancient images.

First of all she is the Mother of God, who is the divine Child with whom she is pregnant. As she is giving birth to the cosmic principle of light, its cosmic counterpart is also called into existence. The Apocalypse symbolizes it as the "serpent of the ancient times." "His tail swept down a third of the stars in the sky." To signify his complementary role in relationship to the light-principle which is about to be born, "the dragon took his place in front of the woman who was about to give birth to a child, so that as soon as she did so he might devour it." (All quotations are from Revelation, Chapter 12)

Our culture has nurtured dualistic thought-forms over long centuries, but we should not let them succeed in 'devouring' the profound meaning of this image. Let us remember that when we consider the core of the universe, we have to do with archetypes that are neither good nor bad. Remember, for example, the yin-yang symbol. This is close to identical with the image of the woman giving birth to the light principle while confronting its opposite, the principle of darkness. Is there not within the yin-yang symbol the same opposition and complementarity of white and black, and does not the yin-yang represent the principle that drives the dynamics of life? The presence of the Virgin with her divine Child is only powerful enough to move the universe if it is resisted by the powers of the equally divine Dragon. How does it happen that we can accept the principle of synergy if it represents itself as a symbol from a distant culture, yet when our own heritage is concerned we think we are confronted by a dangerous enemy that must be eliminated?

When I went on retreat in September 1999, I did not only have conversations with Julius, the old sage from the world of nature. While I was contemplating that initial vision at the center of the Apocalypse, "the figure of a woman clothed with the sun, with the moon under her feet, and a crown of twelve stars upon her head," I came into profound discourse with the Goddess principle within me.

I was most amazed by the way her presence instantly

changed my attitude towards the beast called the "huge red dragon." I felt free to accept it as a symbol of the centripetal powers of the universe which are pulling life back to the center of the centers, that which we used to call no-thing. Their dynamic opposites are the centrifugal powers of love that are initiating expansion and growth.

I do not say that the forces of darkness are not dangerous. Our human experience shows how destructive they can be if they are split off from the wholeness and their role in the cosmic order. But then too, the powers of love tend to become shallowly romantic if they continuously maintain a one-sided optimism.

Next morning, following the symmetrical composition of Revelation, I continued my exploration of its contents by concentrating on the Two Beasts from the 13th Chapter. Looking at them in the mirror of the Goddess within me, I experienced the unprecedented perversion that has been perpetrated on this ageless symbol of the Goddess. I realized that the Two Beasts originally symbolized the life powers of the Virgin incarnate within the earth cosmos. I could have wept with grief when I realized how distorted they appear both in Chapter 13 and in our own experience of them. I remembered how Neolithic figurines often show the Virgin flanked by her two power-animals, which represent her creative forces incarnate on the earth plane. It is not by chance that one of the Two Beasts in Revelation appears rising out of the sea and the other out of the earth.

We will get to know the counterpart of the Two Beasts if we jump to the other side of the central axis of Revelation and consider the Two Witnesses from the 11th Chapter. Just as the Two Beasts represent the earthly powers of the Goddess, the Two Witnesses stand for the powers of the soul, the powers that are working into the structures of space-time from the dimension of eternity. We have already met them in the shape of the powers of the deceased, the ancestors and the ascended masters.

To summarize, when we look at the images that compose the central portion of the Apocalypse, we get to know the Virgin aspect of the Goddess that stands for the totality of life, both cosmic and earthly. She is balancing the forces of darkness, and she is giving birth to the all-renewing consciousness of the universe that our culture knows as the Christ. When she stands between the Two Beasts and the Two Witnesses, the Apocalypse reveals her as mistress of the earthly powers, and of the eternal powers of the soul as well.

In the National Gallery of Slovenia in Ljubljana one can admire a tympanum from the medieval church of the Crusaders, which is one of Ljubljana's monasteries. It shows the Virgin in just such an exalted state. In one hand she holds the golden apple of universal wholeness, and in the other her divine Son[1]. Her throne is positioned over a two-headed dragon and is flanked by two beasts and two tall pillars with doves. The two beasts represent her powers of manifestation and the two doves the eternal powers of the soul.

If translated into the terms of landscape and geomancy, the image of the Virgin depicted in the Apocalypse corresponds to the invisible composition of the 'landscape temples' that are distributed throughout the surface of the earth. They represent the purest and finest layer of geomantic phenomena, the one that gives a sacred dimension to places, landscapes and continents, and finally to the earth as a whole.

To recapitulate our consideration of the geomantic layers, I would remind you that we started by studying the nourishing system of earth's ambience and its archetypal powers. We continued with a presentation of the vital-energy level, and by getting to know the 'chakras' of the earth as sources of its life powers and qualities. Various kinds of power lines and fields complete the tissue of the landscape's vital body. To find even more geomantic phenomena, we proceeded to give our attention to the emotional level of the earth, which we got to know as her consciousness. In this, one can distinguish three layers:

• the all-embracing consciousness of the earth cosmos, which is traditionally called Mother Earth or Gaia and which includes the self-awareness of the planet,

---

1 For a similar example, see the drawing in *Christ Power and the Earth Goddess*, p. 21.

*The Virgin Mary from the medieval Church of the Crusaders
in Ljubljana, Slovenia*

Dimension	Geomantic manfestation (landscape)	Correspondence with the human being
Nourishing system of the earth	sources of archetypal power	archetypal powers of the back
	"dragon power"	sexual power
Vital-energy dimension	Vital-energy organs (power centers)	System of chakras
	Ley-lines (energy paths)	Acupuntural meridians
Planetary consciousness	Sub-elemental level	Subconsciousness
	Elemental beings and nature spirits	Emotional level of consciousness
	Self-consciousness of the Earth (Gaia)	Mental consciousness
Light body	Radiation of the ground (aura)	Auric fields
	Etheric basis of an ambience (the 4 elements)	Light body
Physical body	Matter	Matter
	Geological body of the landscape	Physical body
Worlds of the soul	Underworld	Ancestors
Sacred dimension	Axis of the divine breath	Earth-cosmos connection
	Tripartite structure of the Goddess	The eternal soul
	Archetype of identity	Spiritual identity
Angelic	Angelic focuses in the landscape	Spiritual teachers and masters

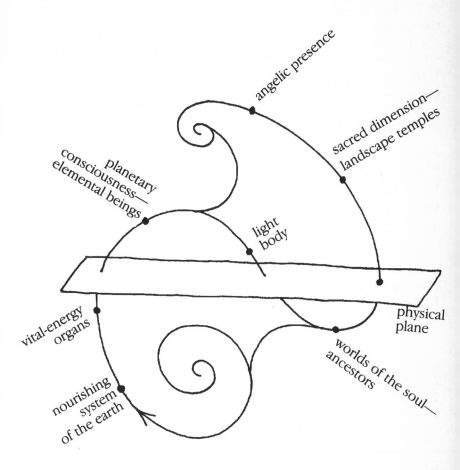

*The model of the earth cosmos as developed
throughout this book
(explained on page opposite)*

- the deep layer of the earth's consciousness where the archetypal powers and images of the earth are stored to support the evolution upon the planet's surface,

- the outer layer of the earth's consciousness, manifested as innumerable elemental beings, nature spirits and devas. They represent the relatively individualized consciousness of plants, animals, minerals, human beings[2], rivers, places, mountains, landscapes, continents, etc.

Next, basing our discussion on the third of the Apocalypse's Seven Seals, we proceeded to explore the earth cosmos by studying the etheric basis of the ambience. We also called this etheric base the light-body of the earth. It is composed of different light sheets, cupolas and spheres that constitute the holon of a place and give stability to its different organs and functions. The various layers of the light-body, as they pertain to places and landscapes, come into existence through the interplay of the Four Elements and their corresponding ethers.

The next step that we took on the path towards the full manifestation of the earth's body was to consider its physical structure, which brings the presence of the earth cosmos to the most tangible level. We did this step by diving into the secrets of the Sixth Seal.

Now, we are about to consider the landscape temples, and enjoy the final chapter of the geomantic phenomena which we have been exploring. But what we meet here as the last could also be considered the first, because we have to do with the most subtle level of the landscape, one that is related to all the different geomantic aspects of the earth. It is the role of the landscape temple organism to interconnect all the geomantic levels we have been discussing, and to complete them by allotting them their unique identity. Through the invisible presence of the corresponding landscape temple, each place or landscape ceases to be just a complicated mixture of different phenomena. It becomes endowed with its own divine core and circumference.

The images from the three central Chapters of the Revelation

2 The natural aspect of the human consciousness is rarely addressed. See my discussion of the personal elemental being in my books *Nature Spirits and Elemental Beings*, p. 199, and *Healing the Heart of the Earth*, p. 103.

of St. John together reveal the principle of the Virgin Goddess, which unites the archetypes, forces and manifestations of the universe. In a similar way, the landscape temples — as the form through which the Goddess manifests her presence in the landscape — unite all the geomantic layers of each place by bestowing on them the mark of identity.

To illustrate how to recognize a landscape temple, we may look at Ljubljana, capital of Slovenia. Over the past several years I have done group work to purify and re-attune its vital centers, its etheric light-body and the different centers of elemental beings that are scattered throughout the cityscape. I have even worked for the Urban Institute of Slovenia to map those centers and their corresponding ley-lines as a contribution to future city planning. By dint of this work, the archetypal form of the landscape temple of Ljubljana finally became settled in my consciousness. I got to know it as a composition of the three components usually found in landscape temples: the axis of the divine breath, the tripartite structure of the Goddess, and the archetype of identity.

By the 'axis of the divine breath', I mean a kind of geomantic backbone such as I described in the previous chapter in connection with the landscape temple of Europe. This backbone connects the inhalation center of the cosmic powers with the center of telluric exhalation. Somewhere in the middle, between the inhalation and exhalation centers, is positioned the third focal point of the landscape's 'backbone'. This is where the divine breath interacts with the corresponding landscape and its life.

This central focal point on the axis of a landscape temple is usually identical with the temple's second aspect, which is its tripartite structure. The central focal point of the tripartite structure concentrates the creative powers of the Goddess as they interact with the corresponding landscape and its life streams. The other two points stand for the Goddess' aspects of Wholeness and Transformation. The places of Wholeness are an expression of the Virgin Goddess, and their function is to ensure interconnectedness within the organism of a place or a landscape. The places of Transformation refer to the Black Goddess aspect and are responsible for guiding life back to its origin. They are places of death, change and resurrection.

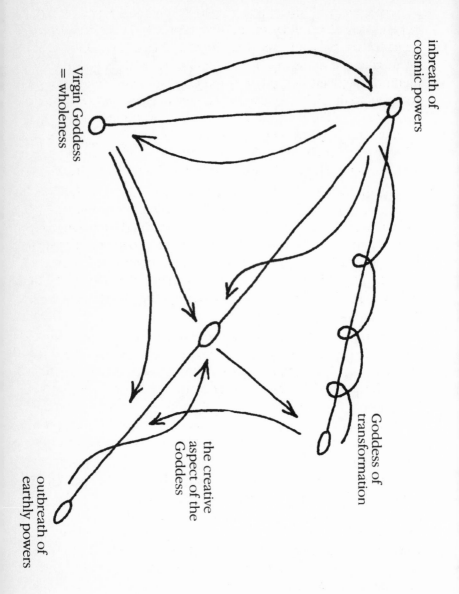

General layout of a landscape temple.

After we, with our group of interested citizens, had worked out the axis of the flow of the divine breath and the tripartite structure of the landscape temple of Ljubljana, we decided to investigate the archetype of its identity as well. Following the method described in the last chapter, we split into small groups and went to the different chakras, centers of elemental beings and focal points of the landscape temple. At a given time the groups simultaneously performed the ritual to mutually link with each other, and followed this with hologrammic-touch exercises and group singing. The whole ritual lasted for about 25 minutes.

At the same time I was watching the inner planes of the Ljubljana ambience for a possible 'sight' of the archetypal sigil[8] of its identity. In my experience the synergy provided by group work of the telepathic kind makes it much easier to perceive a place's archetypal background. For my observation point I had chosen a special place in front of the Ljubljana Gallery of Modern Art. To secure the objectivity of the proceedings, I didn't tell the groups where I would be on watch.

At first, I was nearly overwhelmed by the power of the group synergy that hit me at the very minute the groups started to link with each other as planned. Wave after wave of powerful vibrations followed, and I could feel how the subtle organism of the landscape was gaining strength and clarity as it was approached from different points and levels simultaneously. I was overwhelmed by the power and beauty of life, which usually lies dormant in our perception.

After the first moments of astonishment had passed, I noticed the beginning outlines of a distinct shape. It felt as if the light-form was so large that it would encompass the whole area of the city. Little by little I recognized it as a shell in the form of a vulva. Then I realized that the shell was wide open and I tried to detect its contents. Entering the opening with my consciousness, I realized that I could see a precious pearl inside. Here was a link to the Ljubljana coat of arms, which displays a closed tower on which a dragon sits. For years I have nurtured the intuition that some special power of the Virgin is enclosed within the fortress, and the dragon is there to prevent it being revealed to human eyes. The name of the town, Ljubljana, is also indicative. It is close to identical with the Slovene word denoting 'the beloved woman' – 'ljubljena'.

The pearl, in all its incredible beauty, comes into being through pain. If a tiny piece of stone happens to fall inside 'the tower' of the shell, it causes pain to the living being dwelling there. To round the intruder up and domesticate it, the organism eventually covers the stone with a multitude of pearly layers, a process that results in one of the most precious gems known to man.

I have already referred several times to Revelation as a spherical whole. It grows out of its center in the vision of the Virgin Goddess, Mother of God and mistress over darkness and light. If one continues to study Revelation in this way, proceeding from the middle towards the text's formal beginning, the path will bring the reader to the vision of the male aspect of Divinity. We have already taken this path in our discussion of the 8th Chapter. On that occasion I mentioned that by following the opposite path — towards the formal ending of the text — one would encounter the complementary story. One would get to know the path of the triple Goddess.

Like the story of the beautiful pearl, it is rather sad. After the image of the Virgin or 'white' aspect of the Goddess has been revealed in the central portion of the text, the 17th Chapter of Revelation continues the story with the angel's invitation to John: "Come, and I will show you the judgment passed upon the great harlot who is seated upon many waters. It is with her that the kings of the earth have debauched themselves and the inhabitants of the earth have become drunk on the wine of her filthiness." (Rev 17:1)

Then the angel carried him away into the desert: "There I saw a woman riding upon a scarlet animal, covered with blasphemous titles and having seven heads and ten horns. The woman herself was dressed in purple and scarlet, glittering with gold, jewels and pearls. In her hand she held a golden cup full of the earth's filthiness and her own foul impurity. On her forehead is written a name with a secret meaning..." (Rev 17:3)

These passages introduce a part of the Apocalypse that I used to hate. I considered it merely another portion of the holy scriptures that accuse the feminine principle of taking the human being onto a false path, and so make the feminine responsible for the degradation of world conditions. Yet soon after deciding to ignore these passages, I was forced to look at them again. According to Revelation's symmetrical structure, "the great harlot seated upon many waters" from the 17th Chapter should complement the mighty one "seated upon the throne" from the 4th Chapter. Could she indeed represent the complement of the Christ presence? According to the thought patterns governing our culture, the Great Harlot should rather represent the dangerous forces of opposition that must be mercilessly defeated.

For three days during my retreat I fought with this overpowering thought pattern. Inwardly I felt that the Apocalypse, through its symmetrical composition, was doubtless sounding a most courageous note by putting on the same level of importance the two principles that our culture categorically divides. But my consciousness still put up a solid wall, separating the holy image of the Christ seated on the heavenly throne from the disgusting woman "dressed in purple and scarlet" who is enticing people and seducing nations.

On the third day I got up early in the morning to attune to my invisible friend, the fairy of the olive grove, where I was working on preparations for the present book. My plan was to continue with the theme of the Goddess and address the question of how she appears in Revelation, beyond the generally accepted image of the Virgin from the 12th Chapter. Arriving at the grove, I closed my eyes and opened myself to the place's vibration. Immediately, I was surprised at being inwardly pulled deep down to the bottom of my body. My attention was drawn to a strong, sweet presence pulsating from the depth of my being, as if it was sitting on my pubic bone.

I am well acquainted with the presence of the Christ within me from the years I spent at work decoding the Fifth Gospel. To listen to his voice, I dived into the space of my heart. The path which leads to the core of the heart is safe and acceptable, and I didn't feel any embarrassment when describing it[3]. This time

---

3 For details, see my book *Christ Power and the Earth Goddess*, p. 107.

I was invited to attune to the disgusting space below the bottom of my intestines, though in fact I was attuning much deeper by far. It felt like contacting the very center of the earth.

It was still night and Venus, the Morning Star, was the last star shining brightly in the firmament. Slowly approaching was the day with the most peculiar numerical sign. It was the 9th day of the 9th month of the year 1999, and obviously a day dedicated to the triple Goddess. Because each aspect of the Goddess — the white Virgin, the red Creatress and the black Goddess of Transformation — contains within it those same three aspects of her whole identity, the sigil of the Goddess is 3 by 3, making 9!

Then, from the depth of my being, a powerful voice started to speak to me: "The Goddess gives and she takes away. She gives people countless opportunities to gather experiences and get to know the dimensions of human freedom — without any judgment as to what is right and what is wrong. At the same time she is the one who takes away their heaped-up treasure so that human beings will not forget who they in essence are. Either death or the decline of their inflated grandeur will bring them again naked to their source."

Indeed, if one continues on with the 17th Chapter[4], there is the explanation that was given to John by the angel guide: "As for the waters which you saw, on which the woman took her seat, they are peoples and vast crowds, nations and languages. The ten horns and the animal which you saw will loathe the harlot, and leave her deserted and naked. Moreover, they will devour her flesh, and then consume her with fire." (Rev 17:15)

There is no doubt that the same divine energy which empowers appetites and expectations and gets "crowds, nations and languages" caught up in blind euphoria is also the one which destroys the illusion. It is one and the same Goddess whose power offers humans absolutely all possible types of experience — good and bad — and simultaneously liberates us from being held captive in their embrace. In this last, she traditionally

---

4 The number 17, being the most unsymmetrical and unstable number, is the number of change and transformation. For further explanation, see my book *Landschaft der Goettin (Landscape of the Goddess)*, which is currently available only in German.

represents the black aspect of the Goddess, the Goddess of Transformation, who leads through destruction to liberation and through death to rebirth.

In Christian tradition, the Virgin Mary holding the divine child in her lap usually symbolizes the Virgin principle of the universal Divinity. The Goddess of Transformation can be intuited behind the figure of the Black Madonna. She symbolizes that aspect of the Goddess that accompanies human beings through the dramatic experiences of life, death and rebirth. (See drawing of the Goddess in her totality on page 223.)

So as not to get lost in this encroaching wealth of symbolism, let us remember our purpose. We are not trying to find some order in the endless store of patterns and symbolic names that peoples and cultures have created to help them understand the divine foundations of the cosmos where we live. Neither do we intend to wipe the dust from the ancient images of the Goddess. Rather we wish to obtain insights into the changes in the sensitive relationships between the human being and the sacred dimensions of life which are being initiated by the transformation of the earth cosmos.

Translated into practical terms, the Virgin, as presented in the frequently quoted core chapters of Revelation, embodies the all-connecting, unchangeable and eternal unity of the cosmos. Traditionally she is also known as the White Goddess. Within the human being she would correspond to our spiritual soul, pulsating beyond the limitations of space and time.

On the contrary, the Black Madonna — synonym for the ancient Goddess of Transformation — embodies the divine permission for the human being to forget his fundamental oneness and purity and enter all kinds of enjoyable, disgusting or creative experiences. Even if our identity gets temporarily forgotten and we become fragmented to the point of despair, we cannot get lost because there is a facet of Divinity that accompanies its creation even down to the very worst bottom – and this is the facet of the Black Goddess. And at the same time, through the severe experiences of suffering and death, she liberates us from our dependences and illusions. Translated into the microcosm of the human being, these are the personality generated wishes and concepts that lead us to experience all the possible facets of life, the good as well as the bad. The uniqueness of the personality ensures that each of them is experienced according to one's individual pattern.

It is crucial to understand that the Black and the White aspects of Divinity are equally sacred and equally important to the evolution of life. They are also simultaneously present within each and every life unit. The message of the hidden spherical composition of the Revelation of St John silently urges us not to separate them, raising one up and cursing the other. Both have their role and their purpose within the web of life.

There is even a verse in Revelation with the remarkable number 17:17 that sets out to dispel any doubt about the sacredness of the Black Goddess' role. The passage refers to the "vast crowds, nations and languages" who are slaves to the "Great Harlot" and the "animal" on which she is seated: "For God has put it into their hearts to carry out his purpose by making them of one mind, and by handing over their authority to the animal, until the words of God have been fulfilled." Apart from some unclarity in translation, the verse confirms that to lose one's identity – "making them of one mind" — and to dive into the contrasting experiences of everyday life is to mirror the divine purpose.

Yet the Goddess also has a third face, the image of the universal Creatress, traditionally known as the Red Goddess. She is driving creation forward towards ever-new horizons of strength and beauty. Her main creative tool is the mutual interaction between the feminine and masculine facets of Divinity — or in other words — between the life forces of the universe and its consciousness.

Using Christian language, one can identify her as Sophia, the divine Wisdom[5] and the feminine complement of the Christ. To interlace the impulses of consciousness with the powers of life so as to create a living and evolving universe is indeed a task of profound wisdom. Even nowadays, the divine role of Sophia is valued in the Christian theology of the Orthodox East. In the West her

5 'Sophia' is the Greek word for Wisdom. The Christian concept of Sophia is a continuation of the Biblical Shekina.

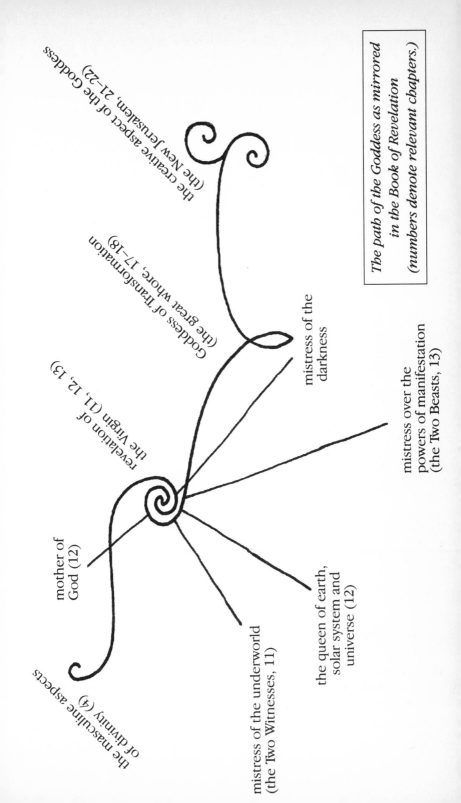

the creative aspect of the Goddess
(the New Jerusalem, 21-22)

Goddess of Transformation
(the great whore, 17-18)

mistress of the darkness

revelation of
the Virgin (1, 12, 13)

mistress over the
powers of manifestation
(the Two Beasts, 13)

mother of
God (12)

the queen of earth,
solar system and
universe (12)

mistress of the underworld
(the Two Witnesses, 11)

the masculine aspects
of divinity (4)

*The path of the Goddess as mirrored
in the Book of Revelation
(numbers denote relevant chapters.)*

presence has been forgotten, and only at the threshold of the Middle Ages did she reappear through the cult of the Holy Mary.

On rare occasions, Medieval and Renaissance works of art depict her with Christ seated on one and the same throne, while he crowns her to make it clear that Sophia is his partner. The Revelation of St. John gives her the name of the New Jerusalem, the bride of the Christ. Such a name is especially precious to us, since we know that the New Jerusalem is a synonym for the transformed earth cosmos.

From its very foundations, the spherical aspect of Revelation constantly maintains a perfect balance between the feminine and masculine aspects of divinity, regardless of whether its story concerns the most sacred or the most profane dimensions of life. By sustaining this equilibrium throughout the whole text, a platform is prepared for the sacred marriage of opposites and the resulting emergence of the new earth cosmos.

In relation to the Virgin, God is first presented as her little child. He represents the self-awareness of the universe born out of its wholeness, which is symbolized by the Virgin. When we continue to follow the spherical composition of the Apocalypse, we are surprised to realize that the Black Goddess from Revelation's right hemisphere has its counterpart in the Christ figure on the throne of the left hemisphere. If she stands for the unprejudiced and uncontrolled experiencing of life, he represents the consciousness that is capable of judging the quality of the experiences gained and defining their proper place in the mosaic of the emerging totality[6].

After the dark aspect of the Goddess and the light aspect of God have been experienced as separate and opposed to each other, as described in the 17th/18th and 4th/5th Chapters of Revelation respectively, the 19th Chapter prepares the setting for their sacred marriage. Listen to the description of the arrival of the bridegroom, coming from the left hemisphere of Revelation to its right: "Then I saw Heaven wide open, and before my eyes appeared a white horse, whose rider is called faithful and true, for

---

6 In this I am deliberately referring to the concept of the Last Judgment, which I understand in the context as presented here.

his judgment and his warfare are just. His eyes are a flame of fire and there are many diadems upon his head. There is a name written upon him, known only to himself." (Rev 19:11)

The symbolism of the verses demonstrates that the 'groom', as already suggested above, represents the self-consciousness of the universe. His riding on a horse indicates that he is a spiritual power, and his faithfulness and truthfulness stand for consciousness' ability to decide and judge. His bride, as his opposite, represents the life streams and the creation of worlds within which life can unfold. So she is symbolized by the form of a city, which is the most complex of life's environments ever created: "Then I saw a new Heaven and a new earth, for the first Heaven and the first earth had disappeared and the sea was no more. I saw the holy city, the new Jerusalem, descending from God out of Heaven, prepared as a bride dressed in beauty for her husband." (Rev 21:1)

Through the difficult process of change, the new earth cosmos comes into existence, carried on the wings of the sacred marriage between two partners who had been lost in opposition and are now about to find their way back to each other. The human being who is rediscovering his partnership with the totality of the earth cosmos represents the sacred ambience where the marriage is taking place.

The continuation of Chapter 21 depicts the New Jerusalem as a perfect mandala, founded upon 12 kinds of sacred stones: "The foundation stones of the wall of the city were fashioned out of every kind of precious stone. The first foundation-stone was jasper, the second sapphire, the third chalcedony... The twelve gates were twelve pearls, each gate made of a single pearl." (Rev 21:19)

Throughout our mutual, and hopefully joyful, endeavor to write and read this book, we have tried to translate the foundation stones of the New Jerusalem — the new earth cosmos — into the practical terms of the renewed earth's aura, the rearranged geomantic systems, the phases of the earth changes, the psychic qualities of the transforming human being, the new relationship to the sacredness of the life cosmos, etc. It is now time to close the book, forget the words, and see what each one of us feels inspired to be and do. But before we part to walk each of us on our own way, let me offer you a farewell.

In October 1997 the earth changes were already under way, but I was not yet aware of their direction. At that time there was an education class on Geomancy and Earth Healing about to start under the auspices of the Hagia Chora School for Geomancy, and I was to lead it together with Johanna Markl and Stefan Broennle. The class was to meet for the first time in Quedlinburg, central Germany. Just beforehand, I immersed myself in my space of inner peace to see if there was anything special that I should tell the group as a sort of starting platform. But when I opened up to my inner space, an unexpected feminine voice, clear as crystal, started to speak to me from within. Only while I was finishing this book did I become aware that I had been given an introduction to the process of the earth changes that were then just about to manifest:

Life is too precious to be squandered unheeded. The earth is too precious to be used up for egotistic purposes. You people are too precious just to glide through life without touching the earth with your feet!

A transformation of consciousness is starting that will reveal to you the deeper meaning of your presence upon the earth. To put it another way, you are going to become acquainted with the true constitution and the true essence of the earth. Both these aspects of the transformation that is currently going on in human consciousness are equally important. One should understand and cherish them in their mutual interaction.

You should get to know not only the secrets of the earth's creation, but also come closer to your true human essence in the mirror of this knowledge of earth's wisdom. The earth accepted you ages ago and enclosed you in her life- and power-systems in order to find in you a partner with whom it would be possible to together lift her creation to a new level of existence. Yet you cannot fulfill this purpose of your being as long as you look on the earth as a mere survival kit, and in consequence, amid all of earth's riches, restrict yourself just to struggling to fulfill your needs.

You are called on to break through this closed circuit of self-denial and earth-insult and take the first steps towards self-realization through your love of the earth cosmos.

Much courage will be needed for you to abandon the old, inadequate images and ties in favor of the new relationship which is now revealing itself between the earth and human beings. It will need much effort for you to re-awaken your forgotten abilities to perceive the earth in its wholeness.

You will need to discover the silent wisdom within you in order to honor the succession of revelations and changes emerging in you and around you, and to see yourself as the mirror of the discoveries yet to come.

You should know that, in its deepest essence, the earth is a heart system and that your real reason for coming here was to awaken the power of love within you. How can you achieve this goal if you harbor no love for your teacher, the earth? Get rid of the old patterns that rule your hearts, get rid of your smart human wheelings and dealings! Life is waiting to be lived in dignity, love and joy.

Updated Report on Earth Changes

Only few weeks after finishing the manuscript of this book a new wave of Earth changes occurred. They started on May 3rd, 2000, when a unique constellation appeared on the sky. All the seven classical planets — Mercury, Venus, Mars, Jupiter, Saturn, Sun and Moon — were concentrated in the zodiacal sign of Taurus. No less significant was the position of two of the 'new planets', Neptune and Uranus, which stood in direct opposition to them. In the course of this dramatic astrological event, the 'old' planets even aligned with each other to form a straight line.

For a long time I had known that nine months after the solar eclipse of August 11th, 1999, when the planets would be forming a cross in the sky, another extraordinary constellation would be appearing. But I had not believed that it could affect the process of the Earth changes as deeply as it did. So I didn't pay much attention to the event. I thought blindly that, having written a book on Earth Changes, I had the planetary transformation process well 'under control'. It took a phone call from my daughter Ana in the late afternoon of May 3rd 2000 to kick me out of this illusion. She asked me if I had noticed that something extraordinary was going on. I went out to the meadows to test the ground radiation. I had become accustomed to the beautiful new quality of the radiation which I had felt emanating from the ground ever since February 1998. To my surprise it had disappeared! The power of the Four Elements seemed to have been broken. The life force of the planet was lower than I had ever known it before.

I thought that the dangerous black-out would only last for a few days — a kind of a shock event. But after ten days I had to admit that the situation had not changed at all. How long could such a black-out last? During the night of May 15th a dramatic dream finally gave me the first insights. In this dream I swallowed my appointments diary, which was of course too large to go through my gullet and so got stuck in my throat. I could neither spew it out nor swallow it. My distress was so great that I awoke. While I was lying awake trying to decode the message of the dream, a silent feminine voice called me by name, "Marko".

I have been called by name in the same way at the start of each new phase in the Earth changes process, so I knew that the dream was a means of making me aware of a new step in the process. My appointments diary tells me where I am to be during any given time-span. Such a diary defines a person's time-and-space position, so it can be understood as a symbol of the space-time dimension in which we are presently abiding. It followed that the dream was telling me that the new phase must have to do with some kind of blockage in the regular structure of time and space on which our 'old' world is based.

Viewed in the mirror of the above-mentioned astrological constellation, the message of the dream appears to be that we are witnessing the first stage of the separation of the 'old' Earth from the 'new'. The situation in the sky, when the 'old' planets were concentrated in the earth sign of Taurus and were separated from the 'new' ones, has obviously provoked a similar polarization within the Earth cosmos.

There was no change in the situation during the following month of June, and throughout I was aware of the loss of vitality in the 'old' Earth. The planet was running on minimum power. But where was the new Earth? Luckily, there was hope. The world-wide 'islands of light', which I mentioned in the First Chapter in connection with Sao Paulo, Brazil, did not disappear. They were the channel providing balance to the Earth changes process, and they became even more powerful.

Successive dreams told me not to panic but to wait patiently. Finally, on July 3rd, 2000, while working with my wife Marika on a lithopuncture project in Biel, Switzerland, I had an intuition that the first stage of the separation of the new Earth from the old one was complete. The image I received in my meditation was that of a snake shedding her old skin. I came to understand that during the previous 61 days the Earth had cast off the first layer of her old constitution. How many layers have to be yet stripped off till the Earth's transformation is complete? Who knows! Speaking in logical terms, one could say that during that 61-day period the Earth has changed her ground frequency slightly. The consequences are foredoomed.

If one is attuned to the old frequency or quality of the planet, one abides on the old Earth. Contrary-wise, to enjoy the new Earth one should calibrate oneself to the fundamentally new quality of the Earth's vibration. On awaking next morning I brought with me the first key for attuning to the new Earth. I did so in this way:

1. Imagine a stream of bright white light streaming through you like a pillar from the universe above to the depth of the earth below.

2. In answer to the penetrating pillar of light, a broad wave of crystal-bright light starts to approach from the depth of the Earth, ascending through your body towards the universe.

3.While both streams continue their flow through you, you should concentrate on your heart center as the point of their union.

4. After a while you should release these images and start to observe the environment, making your heart center your viewing point, or simply enjoy the Earth in her new power and beauty.

After I had concluded the above-mentioned act of attunement, the sensation of the earth's weakness that had bothered me for the previous 61 days instantly disappeared. Instead, I could, without any difficulty, feel the new qualities of the ground radiation just as I have described them in this book, but this time their energy was much more powerful than I had known before. There was the familiar spiraling presence of the Air Element, which is to become the leading element of the new Earth. The undulating presence of the Water Element was so strong that it resembled the roaring of sea waves. If I attuned to the Fire

Element, I became aware of golden bars of light emanating from the ground. The Earth Element shows a crystal-like quality.

If contrary-wise I imagine myself with roots in the earth, and so attune to the earth as I know it from my daily experience, the wonders of these new qualities disappear as instantly as they appeared. Instead, I can feel the extreme weakness of the planetary body and the above-described blockage in the structures of time and space.

As a result of this recent development, right now there are obviously two parallel earths in existence, each pulsating on its own frequency. The gap between them must be so tiny that we usually don't notice it. It is still easy to jump from one level to the other, which is what, subconsciously, we are probably doing all the time. But this may change in the future, after the planet has concluded more such 'sheddings of its skin'.

We will have to learn to attune to the new Earth repeatedly, and finally maintain this kind of attunement constantly, to be sure that we travel to the future and do not get lost within the dead structures of the past Earth. Nature does not know problems of this kind. It simply moves with the Earth through its transformations as part of its cosmos. A vision during an earth healing workshop in Saarland, Germany, made aware of the enormous changes that the nature kingdom has been going through recently. We had finished work on revitalizing the region's vital energy center (solar plexus), when I thought I would delight the group by helping them perceive the elemental beings from the nearby creek, and proposed some enabling exercises. While the participants were doing them, I went aside so as not to disturb them. Thus I discovered a group of ancient alder trees growing in the middle of the stream. Immediately after I had attuned to them, the tall figure of Pan, the ancient God of Nature, appeared in front of me. I was surprised, he was so tall and his presence was so clear. I could have touched him if he had come closer. As he raised his hands I could clearly see the stigmata — the wounds of the Christ — on his hands, feet and in his side. And as I became aware of them — these signs of the Christ that Pan was showing me — silvery beams flashed from each of them to the corresponding points on my body.

The message contained within the vision silently proclaimed that the natural world has in the meantime gone through a transformation that in human terms would signify the incarnation of the Christ power throughout the elemental world. You will remember that in the Eighth Chapter I associated the incarnation of the Christ in the nature kingdom with the symbol of the lamb from the Revelation of St. John. The concluding sequence of the vision could be understood as an invitation to us, as human beings, not to hesitate, but rather to join the beings of nature who are already in tune with the renewed Earth cosmos.

Our natural response might be to ask how we should get in tune with the new, as the nature beings have already done. The present book is full of proposals how to act, and there is no need to repeat them. Yet it should be added that the new phase of earth changes starting on May 3rd, 2000, has also introduced a new task: the transformation and release of old personal and cultural patterns. By this, I mean the emotional, etheric and mental patterns that presently compose what I call the 'old' earth, and the 'old' identity of human beings as well. I became aware of this task during the above-mentioned 61-day period when, in a rather painful way, my personal patterns surfaced, bringing up problems that I thought had been solved many years, and even decades, before. I had to struggle with the same types of illnesses and psychic pressures that I had wrestled with many times previously. But this time, it seems that there is another purpose to the struggle with old patterns.

Within an orderly cosmos it is impossible for a planet simply to throw away its worn-out layer, as it seemed the Earth was doing during the 61-day period that she was 'shedding her skin'. This means that the worn-out structure must be transmuted and reintegrated into the new earth cosmos as soon as possible. The situation that I described as characteristic of the present phase of the earth changes, when the dismantled skin of the old Earth exists on its own frequency level parallel to the new Earth, can only be temporary.

As we work, consciously or subconsciously, on transforming the 'old' skin, we are not only participating in an 'ecological project' — transmuting waste material which are the patterns of the old earth — we are simultaneously working on our personal disassociation from our past identity and attuning to the new. This time the process is not running on the psychological levels but is operating in-depth, i.e. it is transforming our etheric base.

To help in the transmutation process I was shown a simple breathing technique that can be used even in a bus or underground train without upsetting the people around:

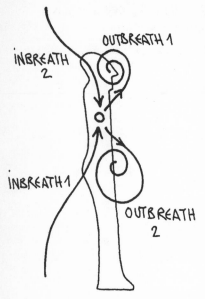

1. While breathing in, imagine that you are taking your breath from the depth of the earth and receiving it through your back, more precisely through the buttocks.

2. Lead the breath upwards through your body to the level of your heart center and pause there for a moment, concentrating on the center.

3. While breathing out, let the breath form a spiral to fill the upper part of your body with the transmuting powers of the earth.

4. Take the next breath from the heights of the cosmos, receiving it through the back of your head and neck.

5. Lead the breath downwards through your body to the level of your heart center and pause there for a moment, concentrating on the center.

6. While breathing out, let the breath form a spiral to fill the lower part of your body with the transmuting powers of the universe.

7. Take the next breath again from the depth of the earth etc.

Sempas, July 24th 2000

Marko Pogacnik